COMMONPLACE MORALISER

Insights and Outrages

Stephen Cohen

UNIVERSITY
PRESS OF
AMERICA

Lanham • New York • London

Copyright © 1993 by

University Press of America®, Inc.

4720 Boston Way
Lanham, Maryland 20706

3 Henrietta Street
London WC2E 8LU England

Library of Congress Cataloging-in-Publication Data

Cohen, Stephen.
Commonplace moraliser : insights and outrages / Stephen Cohen.
p.   cm.
1. Ethics.   I. Title.
BJ1012.C586   1993   170—dc20   92–41784 CIP

ISBN 0–8191–9007–1 (cloth : alk. paper)
ISBN 0–8191–9008–X (pbk. : alk. paper)

Acknowledgements

Special thanks are due to Libi Nugent, who urged me to write this book, and to Denise Grannall, who offered countless comments, criticisms, and insights throughout its writing. A number of people have commented at various stages on particular essays and on the enterprise as a whole. In particular, I have benefited from comments from Jack Nelson, Eric Dowling, David Welker, Ted Cohen, Max Deutscher, and Michael Jackson. Individual essays were read at seminars at the University of New South Wales and at Temple University and Macquarie University, where most of the essays were written during periods of leave from the University of New South Wales. The book is better for the comments received on those occasions.

CONTENTS

Introduction

Let me begin by explaining the nature of this enterprise. To do this, I shall say something about moral philosophising in general — the kinds and levels of concerns which the ethicist might have. And, I will say something about what this enterprise is not. I will explain that what follows is a bit of moral philosophising at a practical level, not at all concerned with what might be called "moral theory" or "moral theorising", and hardly concerned with what have been recognized as "moral issues".

In talking about possible areas of professional investigation or concern, moral philosophers, ethicists, are comfortable with a rough tripartite distinction among —

(a) normative ethics (theories, principles)

(b) normative ethical issues (practical or applied ethics)

(c) casuistry (moralising)

Each of these levels represents a different type of moral concern. The move from (a) through (c) is, among other things, a move from theoretical to practical concerns, and a move from general to specific. At the level of normative ethical *theories,* or *principles,* ethicists concern themselves with formulating and justifying prescriptive principles or moral standards, principles which purportedly represent the foundations of ethics. Utilitarianism (sometimes formulated as "An act is right in proportion as it promotes happiness") is an example of a normative ethical theory, or principle. So might be the Golden Rule — "Do unto others as you would have them do unto you." A normative ethical principle is put forward as a general principle, which is to have universal or near universal application: "People should live their lives according to the Golden Rule."

At the level of normative ethical *issues*, the focus is on the *application* of a principle to some type of general situation or activity which is of moral significance. The issue of civil disobedience, the issue of abortion, the issue of capital punishment are concerned with activities to which a principle might be applied, with the expectation that one could, as it were, reach a stand on that issue. A principle applied to a particular activity of moral concern might yield a result: "I do now hold a position on that issue." Now, let me qualify this a bit. This level, normative ethical issues, is sometimes called "applied ethics" or "practical ethics", both of which names can be a little misleading. If this level is applied ethics, it need not be "applied" in the sense of applying a principle to a particular type of situation or activity. It is not as though, in order to deal with a moral issue, one must be armed with a principle (from level (a)) which has been formulated, articulated, and accepted as justified. Rather, one can, in effect, dive in at the level of an issue itself and work through the issue from a perspective other than that of trying to apply a principle to it. For instance, one might deal with a moral issue purely from the perspective of noticing (or being prepared to be struck by) what of moral relevance is revealed by the issue itself. I won't here go any further with this exposition of the workings of practical ethics. My point is not that of explaining what goes on at that level in lieu of applying a well-articulated moral principle to a moral issue. Rather, my point is only that the respect in which the word 'applied' is more appropriate at this level is the respect in which these concerns (the issues themselves) apply directly to an individual's behavior (rather than the sense of 'applied' according to which one might apply a *principle* to the *issues*). So, it is the *concerns* which apply to an individual's conduct; it is not that *principles* must be applied to issues. And in this respect, sometimes these concerns *do* and sometimes they do *not* apply to a particular person's behavior. This is not to say that the issues are, for that reason, unimportant or that people need not *bother* themselves to hold a position or have a view about them or to be aware of them as issues. It is only to say that as live issues which are actively involved in a person's behavior, they do not all "apply" to any particular person.

Let me say this another way: This level of concern is sometimes called "practical ethics". 'Practical' in this sense means simply "pertaining to action". A practical inquiry is one which is done with an eye toward action. In this sense, normative ethical issues are not, in fact, all "practical" for everyone. Or, in many (I think, most) cases, the respect in which these issues are practical for most people is the respect in which a person might be interested in having the *law* address the issue, rather than a respect in which the person himself is directly involved in or affected by the issue. Even without direct involvement, a person does have a (practical) interest in having the legal machinery address and deal with some of these issues. Or, inasmuch as a person encounters the presence of such issues in newspapers, discussions, television, and talk-back radio, one might well have an interest in being aware of the issues and perhaps even taking a position with respect to some of them. It is in this less direct or less immediate sense that most normative ethical issues would be "practical" for most people. This is a sense somewhat removed from that in which the issues might relate directly to a particular person's activity. It is in this very important, but less direct sense of 'practical' that, for instance, abortion or capital punishment is a normative ethical issue for *me*.

When ethicists deal with moral *issues*, the important thing is to get the moral *analysis* right. If that turns out to be directly "practical" — if it does, in fact, provide practical guidance — so much the better. But if not, that does not diminish the significance, let alone legitimacy, of the moral concern with and treatment of the issue. At the end of her superb article on abortion, Judith Thomson notes quite expressly that she has not provided practical guidance, or a practical solution to the problem. Indeed, she says, "I am inclined to think it a merit of my account precisely that it does not give a general yes or a general no."[1]

The situation is different at the level of casuistry, or moralising. Here there is no question about whether 'applied' and 'practical' are appropriate. Of course they are. Casuistry is exactly that: it is the exercise of pronouncing, or prescribing, what a person should do in that person's specific, perhaps peculiar, situation. Perhaps the moral advice which is given at this level can be generalized so that it has wider application than

---

1 "The Problem of Abortion", *Philosophy & Public Affairs*, 1, #1 (Fall, 1971), p.65.

to a particular person in peculiar circumstances; but that is by no means the focus of casuistry. The major concern at this level is to be able to say what one should *do*, not merely to say how one should *appreciate* a *general* type of predicament. And the emphasis here is in two places: it is on doing, or behaving; and it is on the particular person. The emphasis is on particular guidance. The moraliser is concerned with something which applies directly to a particular listener — something which has direct practical significance for that listener. It is precisely because Thomson's account deals with the problem generically that it cannot give a 'yes' or 'no' to any particular person's situation. Its strength in terms of dealing with an issue per se is its weakness in terms of moralising.

Aside from being more directly practical and more applied, the concerns of the moralist might often not be so "weighty" as to qualify for the title of "issues". The moralist's concerns are, or at least can be, more mundane as well as more specific, or peculiar, than those of one who is concerned with moral *issues*. What I will be doing in the following pages either is at the most practical level of dealing with normative ethical issues or it is right at the level of casuistry. I will, in fact, be offering prescriptions about how to interpret or react or behave toward some garden-variety situations which, I will suggest, have something of a moral flavor. Inasmuch as they are largely garden-variety situations, they are situations not merely with which most people are familiar, but with which most people can directly relate. They are largely situations which most people would directly encounter.

Philosophical presentations are usually concerned to present a thesis, to mount some sort of argument, and to justify some conclusions. Here, however, I want to go one step further and offer some word of justification for the whole enterprise itself. That is, the philosophical legitimacy of an enterprise such as this one, as well as its particular arguments and conclusions, might well be called into question. In case it is not clear from what I have already said as to why someone might think this, I shall say just a bit more about it, and then proceed to offer a *very* brief word of justification.

Casuistry is moralising; and, so the standard line runs, the ethicist, or moral philosopher, has no particular credential or license to engage in this business, which is the legitimate terrain of a rabbi or a priest or a social worker or perhaps a marriage counsellor. Basically, ethicists do and should steer clear of moralising. Not only is moralising an activity for which the ethicist is not particularly well qualified; it is also an activity of little philosophical interest or potential fruitfulness. That is the official, traditional line.[2]

On the other hand, a consideration of occasions which allow for or, perhaps, stimulate moral evaluation might point in another direction. The big issues, and the ones to which the theories are most easily (and certainly are most usually) applied,

---

2 And, despite the presence of those groups of philosophers who came to be known as "the British Moralists" and "the Scottish Moralists" of the eighteenth century, and despite his own approach and concerns, it is a line which apparently caused David Hume, the most famous and influential member of those groups, a fair bit of concern and worry.

are wrongs like murder, theft, and assault — basically heavy, seriously culpable moral offenses — or else issues like abortion, euthanasia, and civil disobedience. However, as I have already suggested, it is not often that, in the most practical terms, we come face to face with these terribly important issues. One might say, then, that we don't come face to face with enough morally significant material to allow us to do much real moral analysis; we don't get much opportunity to practice or to hone our skills at moral theorising or to develop our moral sensitivities. It is only a short step from here to the view that, therefore, moral matters do not, by and large, affect us directly very much. That is, from noticing that we do not often come face to face with the heavy moral issues (real sins), one might conclude that "therefore, we should appreciate that we are ill-equipped for and ill-practiced at moral judging; and furthermore, it doesn't matter much, because, in fact, there is very little close-to-home moral judging to be done, anyway." Alternatively, however, we might recognize that the arena for most moral encounters is different from that in which we meet the gravely serious moral offenses and issues; and so we might realize that the topics about which most moral discussion or moral judgment occurs are basically much more mundane or pedestrian. Perhaps we should say that they are more matters of "manners". That is, from the same premise, that we don't often come face to face with heavy moral issues, one could (and I suggest that we should) conclude that "therefore, we should notice and open up for discussion and analysis what it is that, in fact, occupies a good bit of our moral judging and constitutes most of our moral encounters". And these things, for the most part, are not even on the same plane as the grave, seriously culpable moral offenses. They are much more common, and they are things with which we are much more familiar — things with which we are much more personally, or directly, familiar. Nevertheless, they are *genuine moral concerns*. I want to say this in two ways: one way with the emphasis on 'genuine' (*genuine* moral concerns), and another way with the emphasis on 'moral' (genuine *moral* concerns) — because I anticipate some antipathy with both parts of the emphasis (both that the concerns are not genuine, i.e., that there is nothing, really, to be concerned about, and that the concerns, if there are any at all, are not really moral ones).

There are at least two different kinds of targets or goals of this enterprise. In some cases, I simply point out the presence of a moral feature which might have gone unnoticed. I suggest, in some cases, that a situation or occurrence should be understood in a certain way, so that its moral character becomes apparent. In other cases, the analysis is aimed at offering something of a prescription for behavior.

I think it is important to make something else clear here, as well. Throughout, I am by no means claiming to be identifying moral *truths*. The foundations or the strength or the acceptability of what I suggest does not come from its being *true*. It comes, rather, from being attractive in some other way. (I hesitate to say that the following analyses derive their acceptability from things like "explanatory force" or "simplicity" or other philosophically rooted notions which are invoked to support a theory or hypothesis.) The basic idea is that I shall offer some ways to understand some relatively common phenomena or occurrences which, I think, in their own ways, have some moral significance; and if I were subsequently asked how I know that what I've said is true, my only response would be to say that

I don't for a moment know it to be true, but that I was never claiming that truth was a target of the analysis.

I want to give an example (of sorts) here. One of the topics I will discuss is what I call "vicarious pride", a person's taking pride in the actions of someone else (perhaps a father's being proud of his son). In offering what I claim to be my insight about this phenomenon, I offer no argument at all, and I base my conclusion on a very simple and vulnerable assumption, viz. that any kind of pride must be directed at oneself. I suggest that, given this assumption, there is a problem about understanding vicarious pride, and that, given this very same assumption, there is a solution to the problem. I never, however, offer any support whatever for the assumption. Basically the only support I have for it is that that's how it seems to me; and I assume that you are enough like me so that it will seem that way to you, as well, once I call it to your attention. All I am doing is laying it out for you, and relying on your recognition — and I am relying on it touching a sympathetic chord in you — in order to capture your acceptance. (Of course, your acceptance can take the form — and I would welcome its taking the form — of your reacting with a sigh and the exclamation, "Oh yes; ain't it the truth!")

I hope not to have given the impression that my topic is more lofty than it is; or that I *think* it is more lofty than I *do*. I am going to talk about some very common things, and I am going to offer what I claim to be insights about them. I am going to do several bits of moralising which cover a diverse range of topics. Each bit of moralising stands as a short, independent essay. I begin by discussing the very commonly proferred excuse for failing to do something, viz. "I'm too busy", and I add to this discussion a note about the criticism that someone is wasting time. In *The Derogatory Erstwhile Fact,* I talk about why it is that a certain kind of derogatory remark is, in fact, derogatory. I call attention to a use of language — a pejorative use — where things are not as they seem; where a speaker might suggest that he is using words in a descriptive way, but where he is actually using them pejoratively. In *Justification/Explanation and Treatment,* I call attention to a type of situation in which two people are trying to engage in a dialogue, but because of their radically different perceptions of what the topic of their discussion is (or should be), any dialogue between them is frustrated. *Vicarious Pride* suggests an understanding of what is involved in one person's taking pride in the achievements of someone else. In *"Women's" Gymnastics,* I argue that there is something morally objectionable about the competitive sport of women's gymnastics. The topic in *Vocations and Vocations* is a perception of how some people either do or should view their own occupations and their relation to those occupations. In particular, this essay discusses why it is that when some people dislike their vocations, they are seen to be worthy of reproach for that very reason. And finally, *The Last Word* deals with the ethics of receiving help from someone else. Good Samaritanism is morally praiseworthy. Receiving from a good Samaritan is something which, itself, can be done in ways which are morally proper or morally improper.

Too Busy

It is not uncommon that the claim, "because I'm too busy" is offered as an excuse or as a justification, usually for simply not doing something, for neglecting to do something, or for an act of omission. As with any other excuse or justification, people offer it when there is a presumption that, morally speaking, they should have acted differently from the way in which they did, in fact, act. "I'm sorry I haven't written lately, Mother, but I've been just so busy that I couldn't get to it." "I'd like to do it, Sam, but I'm just too busy right now." "I wish we could get together, but the fact is that I'm so busy these days that I can't see my way clear to do it."

It is clear that "I'm too busy" is offered in order to get the speaker himself off the hook. It is also clear what hook it is supposed to get him off. Now, what, in fact, is this claim saying, and how does it (or how is it supposed to) work as an excuse or justification? We can ask this of the person who offers the claim. Then, there is the recipient of the claim, the one to whom it is offered. What is it intended that this person think? And, on the other hand, why is it that the recipient might well feel slighted or hurt by the "busy" claim or find it generally irksome, even if legitimate or acceptable to him?

"I can't do X because I'm too busy": The speaker is saying that he has a lot on his plate, that there are a number of things which have claims on his time. Because of these things, he says, he can't manage X in addition. So, the speaker is telling his listener, he simply can't get to X, because of these other things.

They are standing in the way, preventing him from doing something which, otherwise, he would do. And there you are: The speaker has explained why he plans not to do X — because there are these other things that he will be doing instead — and he has offered an excuse for not doing X, a justification for taking care of these other things and not X — namely, the significance of the fact that these other things have claims on him. After all, he can't do *this* if he's occupied doing *that*; and, all things considered, he mustn't neglect to do *that*.

Very rarely is it the case that a person has a schedule of activities or an ordering of activities completely imposed on him. It may be that some things or some people or some activities can, all by themselves, constitute claims on an agent ("I can't come over this afternoon, because I'll be saving a drowning child" might have that status); but it is rare that those things or people or activities come already arranged in a hierarchy of importance, or that they, by their very nature, arrange themselves. No; here it is largely up to the agent himself to order these things. And the agent orders them according to some criteria, having regard for concerns such as the importance, obligatoriness, urgency, perhaps pleasantness of the claim, together with his own desires, preferences, and so forth. "I can't do X because I'm too busy" says, then, that of the speaker's priorities (or of the things that the speaker regards as having claims on his time), X comes low enough that by the time he gets to it, there is no time left in the day. X does not put itself at that level; the speaker puts it there.

The importance of recognizing this is the appreciation that "too busy" is not so much the result of external imposition as it is of internal ordering — one's own priorities. In the nutshell, then, the excuse reduces to something like, "I can't do X because

I don't rank it high enough on my list of priorities to warrant my doing it." Stated like this, of course, brings into question the status, or "real significance", of the 'can't' in "I can't do it because I'm too busy"; and it might well make one wonder about the status of ". . . I'm too busy" as an excuse at all. Still, all of this is not to say that "I'm too busy" cannot ever be a legitimate, acceptable excuse. What it is to say is that in appraising "I'm too busy" as an excuse, one should recognize that rather than being externally imposed, its focus is basically one of self-imposition, according to the agent's own priorities. "Because I'm too busy" is misleading, in that it tends to call attention to all those "things" which make the speaker so busy, the menu of impingements on the speaker. What I am suggesting is that, more appropriately, this excuse should call attention to the agent himself — it says at least as much about the one to whom it applies as it does about the things which impinge on him. At least as much as referring to all that this person has on his plate, it speaks about his putting those things there and his not leaving or allowing room for something else, and his unwillingness to make room for this something else.

This is not to say that the impingements which make for one's busy-ness can be nothing but of one's own making and nothing but a straightforward, obvious expression of one's own immediate preferences. What I am suggesting primarily is that the focus of the excuse should be shifted a bit. "Because I'm so busy" does not so much point at some thing or things external to me as being responsible for my situation, as it points to me. More than things external to me, *I* am the place on which to hang the responsibility for my busy-ness. The focus of the excuse (and I do not deny that it can be, or at least can front for, a legitimate and a good excuse at times) is the speaker himself.

An offputting feature of the rhetoric of the excuse is that it tends to indicate that the speaker himself places the responsibility elsewhere: "Don't look at me; look at all those things which make me busy"; and "I'm sorry, but I just can't help it; I'm terribly busy." As a general rule, more likely than signalling a literal external imposition on the speaker, "I'm too busy" should signal that the speaker himself has taken on a lot, and that he orders this stuff in a certain way. By and large, the focus should be on this; the agent should not try to pass the buck.

More than constituting an excuse in its own right, "I'm too busy" says that I rank things in a certain way, with the result that I can't get around to doing the thing you are asking about; and, presumably, I am prepared to present a justification for my ranking things in this way. That is, it says that there is a justification for my ranking; but it itself does not justify it. Being too busy is not itself the justification or excuse. Rather than being an excuse itself, it should be taken — if it is taken at all seriously — as indicating that the speaker has an excuse which he could elaborate if called upon. It itself is not the excuse. It is more on the order of a preface, which says either, "I do have an excuse — take my word for it"; or it invites the listener to ask to listen on to hear the excuse, which at least could be forthcoming if requested. Rhetorically, however, it certainly does not invite the listener to ask anything additional at all. Its function is quite the opposite. And this is at least one offputting feature of "I'm too busy".

Let me be a bit more explicit about external and internal imposition. If it were the case, for instance, that the natural environment were so hostile and formidable that all of a person's energies were necessary just in order to keep himself alive, then the focus of "I'm just too busy to make it to dinner tonight, Mother" would rightly be on those things which are externally imposed on the agent. Through no choice of the agent's own, those things simply are impingements to such a degree as to allow the agent no time for anything else. Another (*the* other?) extreme could be a situation something like this: Bob really goes for relaxation, intense relaxation. He lies in his hammock for hours on end, blissfully enjoying every minute of it. There is, in short, nothing he would rather do; and anything else that he ever does, he views as taking time away from his relaxation. When Bob says it, then, "I'm just too busy to make it to dinner tonight, Mother" reflects on nothing but his own preferences. Here it is a matter of internal, not external, imposition. His offering "I'm too busy to make it" amounts to little or nothing more than if he were to say simply, "I'd rather not come."

Notice that "I'm too busy" does, in fact, appropriately apply to both these extremes. Between them, of course, there are gradations of external and internal imposition. Unless the item of concern is at the one extreme, however, "I'm too busy" does not refer solely to external imposition, and so, on the one hand, the agent himself has something to do with ranking it above those things he professes to be too busy to do, and on another hand, because that is the case, "I'm too busy" does little more than indicate that the speaker himself has ordered things this way and, apparently, stands prepared to explain and justify the ordering. Unless it is offered in the "natural-environment-prevents-me" sense, "I'm too busy", all on its own, neither justifies nor excuses anything; it is, rather, a statement about one's own ordering of priorities. And if that's all that the speaker has to offer in the way of an excuse, then, in effect he has nothing at all to offer: "Given my ordering of my priorities, I can't do X". The fact that it is presented as though there is something to offer as an excuse, and the fact that it masquerades as being the excuse itself can be, at the least, misleading, and, as often as not, offputting.

Far from having defeated the presumption that, morally speaking, the speaker should be doing something different from what he plans, "I'm too busy" might itself provide fodder for a bit of indignation on the part of the listener:

> "Do you really think I can be fobbed off so easily? There was a presumption that you should do X; and, in offering the too-busy excuse, you have indicated that you recognize the presence of that presumption. Otherwise, you wouldn't be offering an excuse for not doing X. You now say, in effect, that you are not going to do X because there are other things which are more important to you or which you would simply prefer to do. And you say this to me as though I should take it as an excuse, excusing you from doing something which we agree there is a moral presumption in favor of you doing. So, do you or don't you have anything more to say than simply that you're so busy? If you do, let's hear it. After all, we both now understand that 'too busy' itself alone really asserts hardly anything. If you don't have anything more to say, then admit it; don't represent your situation as something it is not, viz. excusable."

A Note on Wasting Time

On its own, the "I'm too busy" excuse is pretty hollow. It does not tell the listener much at all about what the substance of the excuse is (if, indeed, there is an excuse at all). It does not tell the listener what it is which is standing between the speaker and his doing whatever he would do if he were not so busy — i.e., what the elements of the speaker's busy-ness are. He offers the excuse, and the excuse simply does not do much — and it might even annoy the listener. The proper filling out of "I'm too busy" would amount to a list of activities and an explanation as to why the speaker cannot or will not find room in that list for the activity for which he claims to be too busy. A list (a hierarchy of priorities) and no time remaining (or no space to squeeze you into the list) are the two central implications of someone's offering you a "I'm too busy" excuse. With respect to these two central features, there is a similarity between this as a purported excuse, and a certain criticism which is sometimes levelled against some people — viz. "He is wasting time."

First, let me indicate what, as a criticism, this is not. (1) "I wasted all afternoon looking for my pliers, only to discover that all along they were in the toolbox, right where they belong." This person is annoyed that he spent time doing something which, had he been better informed, he could have avoided and which he would have wanted to avoid. The time he spent looking for the pliers had nothing else to redeem it. It was simply wasted. This speaker's comment may not be a criticism at all. More likely, it is a lament at an unfortunate situation. If it is a criticism, it is probably a criticism of his forgetfulness, not of his time-wasting. (2) "Poor old Bill: He's just wasting his time trying to restore that ramshackle cottage. It's too far gone to save; and even if he could save it, it still wouldn't be worth living in." In both these cases, the speaker's concern relates to a particular occasion and needn't be a criticism at all. Most importantly, these are situations where, explicitly or implicitly, it is suggested that the time-waster himself could appreciate that he is, in fact, wasting time. The time-waster himself would, or could be brought to, recognize that what he is doing is not worthwhile, that it does not satisfy even his own aims or goals. It is not what he himself would want to do, if he were better informed.

The respect in which some comment on "wasting time" is warranted is the respect in which it is directed as a criticism toward someone besides oneself, and, more often that not, as a criticism of one's dispositional or customary behavior, rather than of one's behavior on a particular occasion. It is offered as a particularly adverse comment on someone else's aims themselves, or on someone's style of living. It is to say that regardless of (and probably quite contrary to) what this person thinks (or even what he could be brought to think), he is frittering away his time. His aims — not merely some particular project — are simply not worthwhile. In any reasonable or justifiable hierarchy of priorities, those items which, for this person, score high enough to move him to action are, in fact, simply not worth doing. In a word, he is wasting his life away.

"Too busy" is an excuse which one offers of oneself. Time-wasting is a criticism which one offers of someone else. Centrally, there are two respects in which this criticism is similar to the too-busy excuse, or rather, is the other side of the coin from that excuse: (i) The time-wasting criticism, like the too-busy excuse, carries a lot of baggage along with itself. By itself, it does not adequately constitute a criticism at all. One is wasting time only if one could be spending one's time on something better. So, implicit (but nevertheless central) to the criticism is an evaluation of someone's activities relative to other activities which are possible for that person. (ii) In recognizing a hierarchy of preferences, the wasting-time criticism implies not merely that the target person's preferences are not the same as the criticizer's. In addition, it evaluates them morally as significantly unacceptable.

As I noted in discussing "too busy", there may be some (few) possible activities which come clearly and unequivocally marked, "Do me!" But, as I suggested, it is by no means clear that there are all that many which do. And, if the criteria for deciding what to do and what not to do are, by and large, nothing but one's preferences, then, almost universally, the "wasting time" criticism will be out of place, just as is the "I'm too busy" excuse.

The Derogatory Erstwhile Fact,

or

Calling a Spade a Spade

"I simply can't understand why he got so upset and, particularly, why he remains so upset. I called him a bastard Jew. So, alright, maybe that would upset him a bit. Still, for the sake of restoring harmony I was willing to apologise for calling him a bastard. But, what's to apologise for in calling him a Jew? He is one, isn't he? So, why should he get so upset when I identify him as one? What could he be thinking in getting upset and indignant with me over this?

"Is he trying to pick a fight? Is he so oversensitive or guarded that he reacts to something that's not really there to react to? The only thing that would make any real sense of his remaining anger would be that he wanted his Jewishness to remain a secret for some reason — perhaps, *ahem*, he's ashamed of it. But then, it's he himself, not I, with whom he should be upset. After all, why should he think there's anything wrong with being a Jew; why should he be concerned that his religious persuasion not be made more-or-less public, or not even be mentioned? Or, more to the point, why would he think that I should know of his desire not to have this fact about himself mentioned? Boy, what a strange and touchy guy! And what a big chip he's carrying on his shoulder! It's such a big chip that it's confusing him about what is the real cause of his anger. (Maybe I should go set him straight.)"

There are two parts of this fellow's story, and they are both worth some comment. The central part is the first part, where I imagine that with a plaintive, innocent look, he raises the question of what makes his nasty remark nasty. The second part, too, is worth saying something about. Here, he sees himself as loosening his kid gloves just a bit, entering the arena of logical argument, and ever-so-politely pointing out that the exchange has, in fact, been more revealing of the offended Jew than of himself, and that it has called attention to an inappropriate or misdirected response to his remarks.

Let me discuss the first part first. Why is it that 'Jew', as well as 'bastard', in "bastard Jew" is nasty? The short answer to this question is that 'Jew' is used here in a pejorative way, and it reveals that the speaker carves up the world in a certain manner, so that it is seen as significant in his negative evaluation of someone that that someone is a Jew. It is not merely that this person sees Jewishness as a significant feature in the identification of any person for the purpose of proceeding to evaluate that person. Rather, he perceives it as a significant derogatory feature itself. Otherwise, the utterance "bastard Jew" either is not appropriate or else simply makes no sense at all. Try, for instance, substituting for 'Jew' the name of some other possibly relevant but value neutral group to which this person might belong. E.g., "You bastard human being", "you bastard civil servant". Either the identification is relevant, in which case it is used pejoratively, or the identification is not pejorative, and the utterance is, at best, momentarily puzzling, and then recognized as just plain silly or nonsensical.

It seems to me that the case might be a bit different if the utterance included 'of a', as in "you bastard of a Jew" or "you bastard of a civil servant". Here, given some circumstances (i.e., given the right story), some credence could be given to the claim that the identification of the person with a certain group does not, by itself, necessarily amount to a negative evaluation. Perhaps, however, it would still be appropriate to call the speaker onto the carpet for indicating that membership in some particular group (e.g., civil servants) is significant for singling out in the context of an evaluation. Perhaps he should nevertheless be called to account for indicating that a standard can be applied significantly to the designated group, that that group can itself be seen as relevant in any way at all which leads to or forms part of an evaluation of this person — as in, "Relative to other civil servants, you're a bastard", or "Measured against the criteria which determine bastardity among civil servants, you're a bastard." Still, this would be different from the speaker's using that membership as pejorative itself. And this would be a different story; not one which applies to the speaker here. Let me, then, return to the story which does apply to the speaker here.

In the use of the phrase "bastard Jew", 'bastard' functions only to call attention to the speaker's regard for Jews. It does not function to somehow isolate and evaluate some particular member of the class, Jews — in the way that, for example, "bastard of a Jew" might, given the right story. And, it is not that the listener is seen to have two objectionable traits — being a bastard and being a Jew. It is overstating things just a bit to say that in its use here, 'bastard' serves only to highlight the derogatory use of 'Jew'. By no means has the speaker here done the two things he claims to have done — viz. (1) say something nasty on the order of "you're a bastard", and (2) quite independently, in terms of logic and meaning, point out that the listener is, by the way, a Jew. The utterance simply does not work that way. As I have suggested, either the utterance is utterly inappropriate for this purpose, in that it juxtaposes things which do not fit together at all comfortably, or it becomes just silly or nonsensical when this structure is imposed on it. What makes the speaker's nasty remark particularly nasty, then, is that it calls someone "Jew" in a derogatory way; not that it calls someone a bastard. It points to what the speaker thinks of Jews, namely, that they're bastards. The remark is particularly, but not doubly, nasty.

In this respect, oddly enough, the speaker is right when he says that he has only one thing to apologise for. Ironically, however, the thing calling for apology is the part of the remark which could be purely and solely descriptive if used in a different context. That is, the particular nastiness of the remark is that it calls a Jew "Jew", and not that it calls some particular Jew a bastard.

When the speaker decides to offer up as clever a complaint about the non-acceptance of his apology (solely for his use of 'bastard'), he, in fact, compounds his offense. He is simply wrong in his claim that 'Jew' functioned purely descriptively, non-evaluatively in his remark. Still, absence of cleverness, or attempted but unsuccessful argument, alone, is not an offense. The additional offense is that he is now lying. He is making false representation about what he had done or meant in making the remark in the first place. I have indicated that in order to make any sense at all, the utterance must have contained a derogatory sense of 'Jew'. It cannot be merely that the remark might have been meant this way, but was not, in fact, so meant by this speaker — as, perhaps, we could imagine that he was so out of touch that he had used 'kike' without being aware that it was anything other than merely a descriptive term (perfectly synonymous in meaning, connotation, and evaluation with 'Jew'). No, it can't be this. It cannot be that the remark is being taken in a way different from the way it was intended. It cannot be this, because that would make the original remark either nonsensical or utterly inappropriate. Given that, there is no way that the speaker could have used the term in the way which he now says should be inoffensive to the listener. When he says that, with 'Jew', all he did was call a spade a spade, he is, rather, all the more revealing a spade as a spade — viz. himself and his nastiness. His apparent attempt at clever retort is itself offensive, then, because it is phony and, itself, additionally insulting.

There is, it seems to me, something of a continuum of derision or pejoration. The continuum does not pertain to the degree of nastiness. It is, rather, a continuum of the way in which sense can be attached to a pejorative or derisive term. It is a continuum of the way in which pejorative terms, or the uses of pejorative terms, function. It is a continuum of the degree to which a word or expression is used emotively, and, conversely, a continuum of the degree to which a word or expression has any descriptive content. Toward one extreme of this continuum of derision are terms like 'bastard' and 'sonofabitch'. Basically, as terms of derision (these days), they are devoid of any descriptive content whatever. 'Bastard' could apply to anyone who is for any reason at all the target of a derogatory remark. As a pejorative, it could never not apply. It is, itself, an unspecific, utterly non-descriptive expression of pejoration. Never could it be the case that something derogatory or objectionable were, so to speak, "true" of an individual, but that it would be incorrect to think of that person as a bastard (as well). If the person is seen to be objectionable, or to warrant derogation in any way or in any respect at all, then it will not be inappropriate to think of him as a bastard. Used in this way, 'bastard' is simply a bit of pejorative "emoting". As such, it does not describe anything about the one to whom it is directed. Although this word does have some literal, or descriptive meaning (unlike some other derogatory words or phrases — e.g., 'fuckhead' or 'ratbag'), that meaning is not at all involved in its usage as a derogatory term. In its usage here, it is precisely on a par with those terms which have no literal or descriptive meanings.

> Fred: "Hank is a real bastard."
>
> Bill: "No he's not; he mugs people."
>
> Margaret: "Well, I don't know about his being a
>   mugger, but I do know that he's not a
>   bastard; he's a sonofabitch."

Because of the unspecific, non-descriptive, utterly emotive quality of 'bastard' and 'sonofabitch', this conversation simply does not work. Similarly, as a one-person deliberation — an attempt, perhaps, to reach the proper evaluation of Hank — it does not work.

Across the continuum in the direction of more description —
no longer solely emoting — come terms which are no less
derogatory and no less nasty, but which have as part of their
derogatory nature some descriptive meaning. 'Smart-ass' resides somewhere in this area. Perhaps a bit further in the
direction of description, but still in the same general area, comes
'fascist'. These (types of) terms are never anything but derogatory, but, unlike more purely emotive terms (or just more general
and unspecific terms) of derogation, their descriptive meaning
is essential (or, at least, is not irrelevant) to their derogatory
nature. It could, in fact, be inappropriate or incorrect to think of
some certain objectionable individual as a "smart-ass": perhaps
the bastard is no smart-ass at all; or "this sonofabitch is certainly
no fascist — his problem is that he's a smart-ass pacifist."
Despite the more descriptive usage of terms like 'fascist', it is
nevertheless the case, at least for many people, that these, too,
function mainly emotively, with just a bit of descriptive content
present. Even for those people who use these terms primarily
emotively, however, there could be incorrect or inappropriate
uses, inasmuch as the terms are not completely devoid of descriptive content, or literal meaning: If, for some reason, you
found Ghandi objectionable, it would still not be appropriate to
think of him, or emote about him, as a fascist. Nevertheless, the
appropriateness of such primarily emotive usage is not directly
a function of whether the terms are descriptively or literally
correct. Descriptive, literal, or even figurative correctness is not
the determinant of the appropriateness of a term's emotive,
pejorative usage. That is, when the terms are used appropriately,
this is not because they are descriptively, literally, or even
figuratively correct. (I think that some people actually treat
'fascist' this way, so that it is applied and seen as appropriate

even where the speaker would agree that it is literally and even figuratively incorrect, but where its emotive application would be inappropriate only if its target were clearly *anti*-fascist, or perhaps at least *noticeably non*-fascist.)

At the most descriptive end of the continuum of derogation are terms like 'Jew' — terms which in some contexts can be used non-emotively, non-evaluatively, purely descriptively. 'Bureaucrat' and 'communist' are commonly located here. The remarkable feature of the terms which are located at this position on the continuum is that their functioning in a derogatory way requires the presence of their descriptive, or literal, meanings which, by themselves, are value-neutral. In order to successfully accomplish its task, in order to be appropriate, and even in order to simply make sense, 'Jew', in "smart-ass Jew" needs its descriptive meaning, as well as its emotive or evaluative use. But — and this is the point which began the discussion — without the evaluative aspect of this usage, the remark would, equally well, be inappropriate or nonsensical.

And, for the person whose monologue began this discussion, the use of 'Jew' is hardly different from a use of 'kike'. "Smart-ass Jew" is virtually equivalent here in derogatory force to "smart-ass kike". Perhaps, however, unlike "smart-ass Jew", both parts of "smart-ass kike" are independently derogatory. I say "perhaps", because I don't have a strong feeling about this. Nevertheless, perhaps "smart-ass kike" refers to *two* objectionable features, in one of two ways: either "he's not merely a kike, he's a smart-ass"; or "among the various objectionable features of kikes is that they're smart-asses, and I'm now calling attention to that particular feature. In any case, "smart-ass Jew" refers to

no more than one objectionable feature, viz. that he's a Jew —
'smart-ass' simply clarifies or articulates that feature.

'Bastard Jew' simply means "Jews are bastards". Appreciation of this construction renders unmistakable the speaker's
meaning with his remark. When he says, "I apologised for
calling him a bastard, but what's to apologise for in calling him
a Jew?", the answer is, then, that there is plenty to apologise for,
not because of the meaning of the word, but because of this
fellow's use of it. Recognition of this highlights the arrogance
— perhaps I should say "chutspah" — of this fellow in trying to
get himself off the hook. He makes out that his offense has been
only of a certain sort; and in so representing it, he compounds
the offense: he's not merely a racist sonofabitch, he's also a
lying bastard.

Justification/Explanation and Treatment,

or

Putting the Shoe on the Other Foot

Stan: "Dammit, Eric, I don't like the way you've been behaving lately. You've been completely irresponsible. You've promised to do things which you haven't done, and you've put me in a position where I was counting on you to do something, and then you didn't deliver. I'm angry! What do you have to say for yourself?"

Eric: "Basically, Stan, old boy, what I have to say is that your problem is that you've been having troubles at home, you haven't been sleeping properly, and you haven't been eating a balanced diet. You need to take better care of yourself."

I want to comment on what has gone on in this interchange, and I want to focus particularly on why it is so irksome to the first speaker. Stan was starting an argument. He was claiming that Eric had done something wrong, that he had no justification for his behavior, and that he was to blame for something. At the very least, Stan is *accusing* Eric of something. Stan wants to talk about, and in terms of, justification for action, and he wants to engage Eric in talk about the culpability of an agent. In effect, Eric is being invited to step into the argument and deny, in some way or other, the charges levelled against him. For instance, he might argue that he did not do what he is being accused of doing, or that he did it but that he had an excuse, or that he did it and that it wasn't such a bad thing to do, after all. He is invited to either do this or else express some appropriate (moral) response to the accusation — contrition, perhaps.

In no way at all, however, does Eric's actual response accept the invitation to argue or to reply in the terms asked for. Eric ignores the possibility of justificatory moral response, and instead speaks the language of explanation. Apparently, the question of *justification* does not enter in here for Eric; *explanation* is what's on his mind. Perhaps, however — and I will return to this shortly — Eric is not ignoring the possibility of justification. Perhaps he simply thinks that in *this* case it is not the appropriate response or the relevant concern.

Along with the switch from the language of justification to the language of explanation, something else also happens here. And, although I do not think that this "something else" is what makes the situation so irksome to the first speaker (the accuser), I do think it is worth noting. Namely, Eric (the accused) has turned the tables. Whereas in the first instance it is Eric whose behavior is the object of comment, rather than replying to this comment, Eric offers his own comment on his *accuser's* behavior (i.e., Eric comments on Stan's commenting). By itself, however, turning the tables would not be so irksome, or would be irksome in a different way from what has, in fact, occurred. Indignation or outrage at the presumption of Stan to pass judgment on him would be a response of this sort — it would be turning the tables, it would be directed at the first speaker's comments rather than at the *object* of the speaker's comments. Yet, good response or not, this type of response would, in an important respect, be on the same plane as the accusations themselves. Namely, the response and the accusations would all be on the moral, blameworthiness plane. They would all be speaking in terms of *justification* for something. A spanner is thrown into the works, and the flow, or continuity, of it all is interrupted when these terms are not maintained. And it is this — not merely turning the tables — which makes it such an irksome situation for Stan. I want to say more about Stan's situation, but first let me note why this shift, or difference, in terms — Stan's accusatory, justificatory language, and Eric's explanatory language — would not be irksome to Eric.

If Eric *were* to find the difference irksome, it could hardly be because the terms have shifted; because, after all, he is the one who thought it appropriate to shift them. If he found the difference in terms irksome, it would have to be because he thought that Stan's remarks were themselves inappropriate, or rather, that those remarks were the wrong *kind* of remarks to be making. That is, he would think (just the reverse of what Stan thinks) that accusation and the language of justification should play no role here. He would think that discovering the appropriate explanation of the behavior (Stan's, not his) is where one's concern should be directed. On Eric's view of the situation, the behavior which is to be explained is, precisely, Stan's using accusatory, justificatory language. That there is a difference, or that Stan uses justificatory language, is what provides Eric with an object on which to comment. Without Stan's "errant" view of what is the proper object of discussion, there would be nothing which, on Eric's view, warrants an explanation. Eric's view of what is going on is such that even if Stan should persist in his accusatory tone, Eric would view this as an "interesting" and "noteworthy" phenomenon; whereas, Stan views Eric's insistence on explanation as "irritating", "upsetting", and, itself, worthy of "reproach".

It is ironic that for precisely the same reason that Eric views it as interesting, Stan sees it as irksome; and so the difference in types of terms could not be irksome to Eric. That this is so is little more than obvious. After all, "irksome" is a criticism; and in the context here, it is a criticism of an agent for his behavior. And this is exactly how Eric does *not* see the situation.

I mentioned that maybe Eric is and maybe Eric is not merely ignoring the object of Stan's comments. That is, maybe he is and maybe he isn't considering and evaluating the criticisms of him which are being offered. Apparently, he is ignoring them: After all, his reply does not address them. Perhaps, however, he *is* considering them and then offering up his considered response to those criticisms: his considered response is to offer an explanation of why Stan would criticize him in the first place. Either Eric is ignoring the substance of the criticisms or he is, in fact, responding to it in the way he sees as appropriate. It is probably easiest (especially for Stan) to think that Eric is ignoring something or that he has missed the point of accusatory language.

However, that would not necessarily be correct. It might be the case not only that Eric sees what it is that Stan is saying but also that, even so, he sees his response as fitting. Awareness of this possibility could be the beginning of some serious soul-searching for Stan. I shall return to this point.

It is worth noting that if Eric has considered the criticism for what it is, and has appreciated it as such, then his reply is *not* completely on a plane different from Stan's comments. Rather, among other things, his reply is suggesting that Stan has missed the salient features of the overall situation — those features, of course, being *Stan's own* behavior, or disposition to behave in a certain way, rather than Eric's behavior.

Consider this as an analogy: Peter is a psychological patient who has a deep-rooted hatred of his mother. That he hates her is recognized by Peter himself. As a matter of fact, in addition to being able to simply assert that he hates her, Peter can enumerate various features of her which he considers to be hateful. Peter's psychologist might well be interested in the fact that Peter hates his mother — this hatred is an important effect of something. Of less interest might be the enumeration of hateful qualities, which perhaps is nothing but a further symptom of the patient's problem. So, although the psychologist might well allow Peter to hold forth not merely about his hatred of his mother but also about her hateful qualities, the psychologist's response might not address the particular qualities at all. The response might appear to *ignore* the enumeration of her qualities. In fact, however, the reason that the response would not refer to the enumeration is that the enumeration is nothing more than an additional symptom of the same problem; and so, when the problem itself is recognized, further symptoms do not have to be given detailed attention. Presumably (just to complete the analogy), the psychologist could have paid enough attention to the enumeration to be able to ascertain that it was, in fact, nothing but a further symptom. The enumeration, then, was not ignored, even though the appropriate response to it was to address something other than it, something apparently utterly different from it and unrelated to it. In this respect, the appropriate response could, indeed, give the impression of ignoring something of significance. It could give the impression of missing the point. But, as I am trying to show, this by itself does not make the response any less appropriate, and it does not mean that the response ignores the remarks of the patient. It is these points which the analogy is aimed at displaying. In particular, the important point is that a response to something may be the appropriate one, even though (or, perhaps, *precisely because*) it does not direct itself toward that which is most apparently asking for a response. It might well be taking into account something to which it does not obviously reply.

Recognition of this point is, at one and the same time, a bitter pill for Stan to swallow and a further source of outrage for him. It is a bitter pill, inasmuch as Stan should appreciate that maybe — just maybe — Eric is right, that Stan's action of criticising Eric is not so much a comment on and a response to Eric's perceived moral shortcomings as it is a symptom of some physical or psychological malady of Stan himself. Still, Eric's response is a further source of annoyance for Stan, inasmuch as Stan sees that Eric has *unilaterally* decided that his response is appropriate. Even so, however, it is not Eric's making a unilateral decision which is so annoying. Rather, it is his making *this* unilateral decision, a decision which cuts off the possibility of further response from Stan. Anything further which Stan might say would, in Eric's eyes, be merely something else which stands in need of explanation; it would be seen as just another symptom. Eric's response has been to view Stan's behavior (or disposition to behave in this way) as something to be *explained* and then *treated*. This leaves little room for Stan to get the discussion back onto the track of justification and moral, not psychological, evaluation. It leaves little room for Stan to do anything except feel frustration. He wants to do something — in particular, he wants to engage in a dialogue of a particular sort — and Eric won't allow this to happen. (Eric's behavior in all this does not clearly indicate one way or the other whether he would allow and would participate in a dialogue of a different sort, viz. a discussion of the proper *explanation* of Stan's behavior.)

Outrage is Stan's first response: Here he was, wanting to have it out with Eric, and what he met with was worse than a brick wall. Originally, Stan was indignant, critical of Eric. Then, on hearing Eric's response, Stan is outraged and frustrated. He sees that Eric is not allowing him to be on a level equal to Eric's own. He sees Eric as not treating him as a fully-fledged person who knows what his situation is and what he is trying to do. He sees Eric as turning a blind eye to the real issue and to the real *type* of issue, a moral one. On further consideration of Eric's response, perhaps the outrage, but not the frustration, eases somewhat; not because of any resolution of their differences or any solution to the problem, but rather because of further confusion — viz. the thought that Eric's response just might be the right one, but that whether or not it is, it has absolutely stifled the possibility of further discussion.

If this were an occasion for theorizing at a more general level, I would expand on this point, which is basically one concerning what is involved in treating persons as persons, rather than as objects or as something less than fully-fledged persons. I *will* say just a word about it. The issue of treating persons as persons arises in the context of the relation between an individual and an institution (e.g., a government), as well as in the context of interpersonal relations. In the nutshell, it is an issue about dealing with individuals so that their personhood is respected, and so that they are not regarded merely as things to be taken care of or looked out for (as Eric would describe Stan in his situation). It is an issue concerned with allowing an individual the consideration and regard which individuals deserve in virtue of being persons. This involves, among other things, respecting a person's choices — not necessarily agreeing with or accepting them, but regarding them as emanating from an individual with a certain status and certain entitlements. One aspect of the issue concerns how someone should regard and deal with someone else. Another aspect concerns how a person should be able to expect that others will regard and deal with him himself. I.e., one aspect concerns how we should treat others, while another aspect concerns how we should expect to be treated by others. For example, as wrong, cockeyed, and even morally reprehensible as they may be, I should respect another person's choices as emanating from that person himself, as being an expression of that person's free will. This does not mean that I should *like* them or that I should like *him* — or even that I should tolerate them or him. It means only (only!) that I should give that person the proper credit or blame for those choices — that I should consider that person responsible for those choices. And, I should be able to count on other people to accord *my* choices that same status. There should be a strong presumption that a person's choices are his own, that they are things which the person himself does, rather than (like a knee-jerk or a headache) things which happen *to* the person and must be dealt with accordingly.

> "In cases of not treating a human being as a person we interfere with a person in such a way that what is done, even if the person is involved in the doing, is done not by the person but by the user of the person. . . . A person may be grabbed against his will and used as a shield. A person may be drugged or hypnotized and then employed for certain ends. . . . There are affinities between coercion and other cases of not treating someone as a person, for it is not the coerced person's choices but the coercer's that are responsible for what is done."[1]

For the point here, rather than venturing into other areas, such as the issue concerning the humanity of retributive as opposed to utilitarian punishment (an area where "persons as persons" becomes a central issue), I shall leave the discussion at the level of a difficulty encountered by two people who are trying to deal with each other in what each perceives as the morally appropriate way. It is important to note, however, that this is generically the same issue — "persons as persons" — which, at the level of what could be a common discussion, has practical import. One need not turn one's attention to a topic as weighty as punishment in order to run into as centrally important a concern as treating

---

1 Herbert Morris, "Persons and Punishment", in Morris' *On Guilt and Innocence* (University of California Press, 1976), pp.588-589. Reprinted from *The Monist,* 1968.

persons as persons. Stan's complaint about Eric is precisely that Eric is *not* treating him (with his criticizing of Eric) as a person, that Eric is not allowing him to accept — for better or worse — the responsibility for his own choices and actions.

Vicarious Pride

The notion of pride has had a checkered history. Such notables as St. Augustine, Thomas Aquinas, Dante, and Martin Luther all regarded pride as one of the seven deadly sins, along with avarice, lust, anger, gluttony, envy, and sloth. In some quarters, pride was seen to be the very essence of sin. Immanuel Kant, as well, believed that nothing good could be said about pride. For Kant, however, pride's failings were purely moral, and not specifically religion-oriented. According to Kant, pride is a vice which violates a person's duty of respect for other people:

> "[pride] is a kind of ambition according to which we demand that other men esteem themselves but little in comparison with us. Accordingly, pride is a vice which conflicts with the respect to which every man can make a [morally] lawful claim."[1]

Immediately before Kant, things were clearly on the upswing for pride when David Hume suggested that a feeling of pride is not always vicious, just as a feeling of humility is not always virtuous:

> "by PRIDE I understand that agreeable impression, which arises in the mind, when the view either of our virtue, beauty, riches, or power makes us satisfied

---

1 Immanuel Kant, *The Metaphysical Principles of Virtue, 1797.*

with ourselves: And . . . by HUMILITY I mean the opposite impression. 'Tis evident the former impression is not always vicious, nor the latter virtuous. The most rigid morality allows us to receive a pleasure from reflecting on a generous action; and 'tis by none esteemed a virtue to feel any fruitless remorses upon the thought of past villainy and baseness."[2]

Well before any of these moral and religious theorists condemned and then uncondemned and then condemned pride, Aristotle had characterised it as a full-blown moral virtue:

"with regard to honour and dishonor the mean is proper pride, the excess is known as a sort of 'empty vanity', and the deficiency is undue humility"[3]

"[pride] is concerned with great things. . . . Now the man is thought to be proud who thinks himself worthy of great things, being worthy of them; for he who does so beyond his deserts is a fool, but no virtuous man is foolish or silly. . . . he who thinks himself worthy of great things, being unworthy of them, is vain. . . . The man who thinks himself worthy of less than he is really worthy of is unduly humble. . . . The proud man, then, is an extreme in respect of the greatness of his claims, but a mean in respect of the rightness of them; for he claims what is in accordance with his

---

2 David Hume, *Treatise of Human Nature, 1739.*

3 Aristotle, *Nicomachean Ethics*, II, 7.

merits, while the others go to excess or fall short. ... the truly proud man must be good."[4]

The British Moralist and immediate predecessor of Hume, Bernard Mandeville, held that pride is "a certain pleasure [which a person] procures to himself by contemplating his own worth."[5] By itself, this view sounds similar enough to the others cited as to warrant no comment at all. However, even though this definition by itself could sit equally well with Kant as with Aristotle, the moral *status* which Mandeville accorded pride is radically different from that claimed by anyone else. According to Mandeville, "the moral virtues are the political offspring which flattery begot upon pride."[6] Mandeville was, in fact, no particular *fan* of pride. Indeed, he thought it worse than a vice. However, because of the matter of its parenthood and lineage, pride would stand outside the whole area of morality, and so, it would seem, could itself be subject to neither a favorable nor an adverse *moral* evaluation.

Pride is of moral concern. Everyone is agreed about that. And, Mandeville aside, the consensus is that pride plays a dual role in the moral scheme of things. One of its roles is as a moral

---

4 Nicomachean Ethics, IV, 3. Was Muhammed Ali proud (with his "I am the greatest!"), or was he vain?

5 Bernard Mandeville, *An Enquiry into the Origin of Moral Virtue*, 1723.

6 Mandeville, *An Enquiry Into the Origin of Moral Virtue*, 1723.

evaluation (of oneself). It is a moral sentiment. Its other role is as the *object* of moral evaluation (Aristotle thought that pride is a moral virtue; Kant thought that it is morally reprehensible to engage in this kind of personal moral evaluation). As a moral sentiment, whether it is moral, immoral, or sitting on the fence, pride amounts to a certain high estimation of one's own qualities or achievements and a corresponding feeling or attitude toward oneself because of that estimation. We are generally familiar with this emotion and with directing it toward ourselves: "She takes pride in herself because of her wit", or "she takes pride in her wit", or "she's proud of herself because of her achievements". Basically, pride is self-directed.

It is this central feature of pride which brings me to the principal concern of this discussion, viz. an explanation of those cases where pride is apparently *not* directed at oneself. How are we to understand references to phenomena such as pride in one's child, or in general, pride in someone else or someone else's achievements? That is, how are we to understand "vicarious pride", a situation in which a person feels proud not because of something *he* has done or something which reflects on *him*, but rather because of something which reflects on someone else? It quite clearly *will not* do to say that this all amounts simply to one person recognizing that someone else did something well, and that the first person is proud of that other person just because of that. To be favorably impressed (even *very* favorably impressed) with someone or something is one thing; to feel pride is another. Appreciating that someone is doing something well is, in itself, nothing more than being favorably impressed with the person or the person's achievement. This appreciation, alone, does not amount to taking pride in the person or the achievement. Compare, for example, "being impressed with

Torvill and Dean" with "taking pride in Torvill and Dean" (which a fair proportion of the British population would claim to do).

There are, I think, two senses in which one can feel pride because of someone else's actions, two senses in which one can take pride in another's achievements or simply in another person. One of these senses is not really vicarious pride at all, but is, rather, only a disguised pride in oneself. The other sense is more nearly vicarious.

One reason for feeling proud of someone else is that that other person is perceived to reflect directly on oneself. If a particular person's pride in his child is to be understood in this way, then the person is not actually proud of the child at all, but rather is proud of himself. In beaming with pride while her daughter wins the 100-metre dash, the mother is actually proud of her own achievement in producing such an offspring. She is proud in virtue of how this win reflects on *her*. To be an instance of *vicarious* pride, the object of the pride would have to be the win, as it reflects on the child, period. It is not vicarious pride if the object is the child's win as it reflects on oneself, the parent.

How could the parent's pride here be anything else? What sort of understanding or description could we bring to this sort of event so that the pride could, in fact, be something other than the simple, although obliquely-revealed, pride-in-oneself which I have described? (Or, is the only other possibility that the feeling is not pride at all, but instead is simply the feeling of being very favorably impressed by something?)

If one *does* feel pride, then, I think the appropriate description could never ignore one's own position in the whole situation, even if the pride being described was as nearly vicarious as possible. That is, if sense is to be made of how pride can be felt in a particular situation, reference must always be made to one's own position in that situation or one's relation to the other principals in the situation. Otherwise, the feeling would be "appreciation of" or "being impressed by", or some such thing, but not "being proud of". Because of this, I suggest that pride can never be purely vicarious. In this central respect of explicating pride as only self-directed, the traditional views are correct. And so, a claim that Jean takes pride in Sally's achievement always stands in need of a bit of unpacking in order to make clear that in virtue of which the feeling of pride is possible — i.e., to make clear the relation Jean has to Sally which allows her to identify with Sally or Sally's achievement. The relation need not be of the sort I have suggested with the mother and her 100-metre-dash-winning daughter; but, I suggest, there must be reference in one way or another to one's own involvement in or contribution to the achievement.

The other sense in which one can feel pride, the one which is more nearly vicarious, is a sense in which a person recognizes his own involvement as a member of a group. In this way, one's pride in someone else or someone else's achievements is not in the sense of being a causal agent or a producer of those achievements, but rather in the sense of belonging to the group out of which those achievements sprang. The achievements reflect on the group, and inasmuch I am a member of the group, they reflect on me. A different parent might, in this way, be proud of her daughter's winning the 100-metre dash: Here, that which gives rise to the feeling of pride is not the parent's own achievement, as it was for the other parent. Rather, it is the parent's involvement as a member of a group to which the daughter belongs —

namely, the family. The winning run reflects on that group, not necessarily in the sense of its being caused or produced by that group, but in the sense of its springing from and being associated with that identifiable group.

Both these parents feel pride, but their views of their involvement and their relation to the actual achievements are different. A soloist can take pride in a good performance as something that she did. A participant in a large marching formation can take pride in being part of something worthwhile. Between these two extremes — of being the sole (causal) agent and being a member, not really an agent at all — there can be a range of possibilities. But, I suggest, in order for there to be pride, a person must see himself as, in one way or another, being involved with the achievement. One must identify or link or in some way associate oneself with the production or producer of the achievement. It seems to me, then, that pride cannot be understood as purely vicarious. It cannot be, say, purely altruistic or other-directed.

As the link becomes less a causal one or in general less tangible or less direct and immediate, and as the size of the associated group becomes larger or more amorphous, the significance of a claim to take pride in whatever or whomever changes greatly. Compare, in terms both of meaning and significance, the difference among these:

(1) the mother who is proud of her achievement in producing a child who can run the 100-metre dash so quickly;

(2) the parent who is proud of her child's running the 100-metre dash so quickly;

(3)   the citizens who take pride in their country's Olympian running the 100-metre dash so quickly. In considering this sort of case, consider it in two ways — both (i) as the citizens seeing themselves as contributing causally to their country's or the Olympian's achievements, and (ii) as their seeing themselves not as causal contributors but still taking pride in the achievement or in the person of the Olympian;

(4)   someone feeling proud that, simply, *some* person was able to run the 100-metre-dash so quickly. Imagine this person with his face beaming because he sees that yet another achievement has sprung from his group, the human race — "I'm just *so* proud of *just* everyone!"

The vicarious pride of the person in (4) is at best silly (if not bogus or incomprehensible), precisely because the very idea of anyone's being associated in any appropriate or requisite way with the "group" from which this achievement sprang is ludicrous. As suggested by the theorists cited at the beginning of this discussion, pride requires a high estimation of oneself or one's achievement *relative to others*. Among other things (e.g., an identifiable group which is not amorphous), it is the "relative to others" (or "relative to another identifiable group") which is most apparently missing from this person's sentiment. Perhaps the vicarious pride here could be genuine (although no less silly) if there had also been an ape, a mule, and a pony in the race.

"Women's" Gymnastics

I used to think that the high-level competitive sport of women's gymnastics as a public spectacle was so extremely and intrinsically perverse that anyone with moral sensibilities and sensitivities which were developed to even a moderate degree should make a point *not* to spectate: The pleasure one gets from watching the sport is a pleasure that one should try to curb. My present view is not quite that extreme. It is not the case, however, that I have changed my mind about the nature of women's gymnastics. Rather, it's that I am no longer so certain that such a harsh reaction is called for in response to its perversity.

It is not *universally* the case that top "women" gymnasts are young girls. But notice: In 1968, when she was at her peak and had a very strong chance for Olympic gold, the U.S.'s Cathy Rigby was fifteen years old. In that year, the old-timer Vera Caslavska, at twenty-six, won the all-around medal. Olga Corbett was at the top of her game at age seventeen. 1976 was Nadia Comaneci's year. She was fourteen. In that year, Bela Karolyi, who was Romania's (and, in particular, Nadia's) coach, acquired a worldwide presence as the premier coach of women's gymnastics. Maria Filatova took out the all-around in the World Cup in 1977 at age sixteen. Yelena Davydova, another relative oldie, won the all-around Olympic title in 1980. She was a ripe old eighteen. In 1984, seventeen-year-old Mary Lou Retton won. Karolyi had come to the U.S.A. and was her coach. In 1988, Karolyi, who by then had been in the U.S. long enough to truly participate in the development of some American gymnasts, had a couple of hot prospects in Chelle Stack (fourteen) and Phoebe Mills, who, at fifteen, won the all-around at the 1988 U.S. championships. Of course, there are many other experienced gymnasts on the world scene, as well — e.g., the U.S.S.R.'s fifteen-year-old Svetlana Baritova, and Romania's Aurelia Dobre, who, at fifteen, was the 1987 all-around world champion. I could cite the ages of a number of other contemporary world-class women gymnasts. The purpose would be simply to further substantiate the point that the ages are young. Dobre, who was competing with an injury, didn't win the all-around at the '88 Olympics. And, Baritova, who did win an apparatus, missed out on coming tops in the all-around. As it happened, the very old Elena Shushunova (at nineteen) from the U.S.S.R. eked out the all-around from Dobre. It was indeed a year for the oldies. It is significant that with the 1988 Olympics, came a rule that there would henceforth be a minimum allowable age for competitors in women's gymnastics: Entrants must be at least fifteen years old. Actually, they need not actually *be* at least fifteen; it is sufficient that they will *become* fifteen at some point in the year in which the competition is held. Not all competitions have adopted this rule, however. In 1990, Tatiana Liesanko from the Soviet Union won the all-around in the Word Cup, at age fourteen. And, in 1991, fifteen-year-old, 4'7", 80-pound Kim Zmeskal led a U.S. team of thirteen-, fourteen-, and fifteen-year-olds, and took out the all-around at the world championships. By 1992, Zmeskal had won the U.S. championships three times. The all-around at the 1992 Olympics was taken out by fifteen-year-old Tatyana Gutsu from the Unified Team of Former Soviet Republics. Gutsu herself was a last minute replacement for her fourteen-year-old teammate, Roza Galiyeva, who was forced to withdraw with an injury.

In an article in *Sports Illustrated,* Craig Neff referred to Mills and Stack as being Karolyi's "two latest prodigies."[1] That wasn't correct. Their achievements and status, I believe, were not at all prodigious. I think that this is what people like Karolyi have shown. To be a grand master at bridge when you are fifteen years old would be prodigious. So would making it into the NBA at seventeen, or being a member of Australia's Davis Cup team at sixteen, or publishing a philosophy text at age twenty-four. In the sense in which Neff (and most others) use the word these days, 'prodigy' has to do with acquiring success, or reaching a particularly high level of achievement in some endeavor, at a surprisingly or unusually young age. (I.e., 'prodigy' isn't used to mean merely that a particularly high level of achievement has been reached by someone, of *whatever* age.) If this *is* the way the word is being used, then, of course, the fittingness of the notion of "prodigy" will be relative to the particular endeavor about which one is concerned. To be a particularly skillful, world-champion at marbles at age fourteen is probably not prodigious, whereas winning an open darts championship at eighteen probably is. To be president of a bank at age thirty-five probably is prodigious; to be president of your own computer company at age thirty probably isn't (anymore). It is in this sense that I am asserting that the achievement of gymnastic excellence by young teenage girls is not prodigious. Rather, the younger the better; or rather, the younger, the better their chances.

---

1 *Sports Illustrated,* March 14, 1988, p. 73.

Let us assume that for reasons applicable to other sports as well, women's gymnastics is at a higher level than it was, say, thirty years ago. More is being asked of the gymnasts in their routines and in their dedication; there have been qualitative advances in training techniques, sports medicine, and sports psychology; and there is a host of other reasons which support this assumption. Let us assume that the now more frequently achieved scores of "10.00" and "9.95" indicate something other than that the criteria for scoring and for excellence have been lowered or that judges now see through more generous eyes. The scores have gone up; the ages of the top participants have come down (the corollary of which is that the age at which one is over the hill has also come down). And, the ages have come down to such a level that it would be an old-timer indeed who was old enough to be permitted to drive herself in a car to a training session. We are a long way indeed from 1956, when thirty-five-year-old Agnes Keleti won the all-around Olympic gold.

Let us say that, in very broad strokes, there are three distinguishable categories of characteristics which are integral to prowess in this sport:

(1)   suppleness, or flexibility, of one's body;

(2)   muscle development, as it is involved in strength and balance; and

(3)   experience, through learning and practicing.

Even with all the strength in the world, one will not excel unless she knows what to do with that strength and has the requisite physical flexibility. Similarly, to know what to do (both in the respect of one's mind and in the respect of one's body) will not be sufficient for success unless one has the strength and the suppleness to put into effect what one knows, and to do it in a way such that she looks fluid in doing it. And, of course, success will not come simply in virtue of suppleness and a certain appearance of one's body: in addition, the gymnast needs muscle development and experience.

In the nutshell, my claim is that the premium placed on (1), including the *appearance* or *lines of the body* which count toward excellence (present in, for example, the balance beam and the floor exercises), is such as to make pre-pubescent characteristics a preeminent asset, if not positively a prerequisite, for excellence. It is not merely the amazing degree of suppleness which I have in mind in urging this claim. I am also thinking of the particular movements and appearance which are prized and rewarded in a performance. I believe that on both these counts — actual suppleness and general appearance — a "mature" body would hardly be an asset. On the contrary. I am not thinking only of the presence (or absence) of developed breasts and hips; and I am not thinking only of the presence (or absence) of typically pre-adolescent collagen levels. I am also thinking of the lithe figure displayed in, say, floor exercises, where merely (merely!?) performing a routine with technical perfection will not alone secure world-class success. An appearance is required, as well. And, to put it bluntly, that appearance is of a little girl. Pre-pubescent characteristics and demeanor are significant assets in these two respects.

Let me speculate that, given the required combination of suppleness, muscle development, and experience, the optimum physical age of a woman gymnast would be somewhere between eleven and thirteen. What makes any age optimal will be its ability to exploit the gymnast's pre-pubescent characteristics (or her pre-pubescent advantage), while allowing her to have acquired the developmental features of (2) and (3) above — muscle development and experience. I am not claiming that the required characteristic of suppleness is *nothing but* a child's natural ability. *Of course* it is more than that; it is *much* more than that. Suppleness can be developed. What I *am* claiming is that the advantage which pre-pubescent characteristics offer the gymnast — both in terms of characteristics which, themselves, can be developed, *while remaining pre-pubescent,* and in terms of the appearance of pre-pubescence — is so great as to warrant the remark that pre-pubescence is a prerequisite for world-class success. But so what? Even if this claim is correct, how does that lend support to the claim that the sport is perverse? I shall return to this soon.

There have been claims from some quarters that some aspects of this sport (and I am thinking again of floor exercises) are, beyond a certain technical level, non-judgeable. Perhaps they would be judgeable as artistic or perhaps they would be centrally impressionistic; but, whatever, they are not judgeable in any straight-forward or mechanical way. And, they are not judgeable as *athletic,* as distinct from *artistic.* Similar claims have been made with respect to some features of figure skating and ice dancing, both of which require the presence of that "special something" beyond technical merit. That something beyond technical merit is required is beyond doubt in those sports: marks are formally awarded for artistic interpretation; and that must surely include (formally or informally) presentation and appearance. But, one could safely bet, the appearance which is rewarded in those areas is certainly not that of a child. And, I think, the structure and grading of the skating routines is not such as to favor the level of physical development of a child. Quite the opposite.[2] But that itself could be a topic for discussion on another occasion.

Why am I talking about skating? Because it bears a significant similarity and a significant dissimilarity to the situation with women's gymnastics. It is the *dissimilarity* which warrants the charge of perversity being levelled against women's gymnastics but not against skating. The similarity to which I am referring is simply that *appearance* is integral to performance in both these sports. Whether that feature does or does not put the sport into the realm of the artistic or the impressionistic or something else which one might want to contrast with athletic is not important to my point here. (And, any question about whether such an artistic element can, in fact, either legitimately or appropriately be distinguished from the athletic anyway is a question which I am not going to address at all.) The dissimilarity is with respect to the age-relatedness of the requisite appearance, and, as I have suggested earlier, the age-relatedness of the actual physical characteristics which figure prominently in performing. For gymnastics, even if it is not the case that the appearance actually *sought* is to be childlike (and that it *is* is at least arguable), it is nevertheless the case that childlike attributes are integrally important to the achievement of whatever that

---

2 N.B. the appearance, demeanor, and success of Katarina Witt.

"special something" is. Even if the gymnasts are not striving to appear childlike; nevertheless, childlike attributes are important toward their achieving whatever appearance they *are* striving for (however that appearance itself is to be characterized).

(Even) if I am right about this so far, how does this lead to the global-sounding charge that the sport is perverse? Surely an activity is not perverse merely because it exploits or requires the development of a pre-adolescent characteristic in its participants. And, it is not perverse merely because it puts that developed characteristic on public display. I would not claim, for example, that the Vienna Boys Choir is a perverse organization in virtue of the facts that it requires pre-adolescent boys' voices and that it puts those voices on display. Requiring a pre-adolescent characteristic, developing that characteristic, and then putting it on public display do not, by themselves, make the activity perverse — although, I think they do go some way toward it: To invite ogling of a display of a pre-adolescent characteristic on a world stage is already to go some distance toward perversity, both in those who extend the invitation and in those who accept it.

(1) There are any number of activities which children develop and perform publicly. Adults watch, cheer, and appreciate the children's achievements at ballet, baseball, and high-jumping, knowing all the while that countless other people perform those activities to a higher standard. With some such activities, even though no one presently *does* perform them to a higher standard, there is no doubt that other people *could,* if there were any reason, or purpose, or incentive for them to do it — e.g., kickball, vigaro, or Tee-ball. (2) There are some activities which, again, are developed and performed publicly by children

to which no higher standard is appropriate: Once again, the Vienna Boys Choir comes to mind. In activities like this, it is essential that it is a *child's* characteristics which have been developed to a particularly high level. The fact that their performance is not, as it were, in the "junior division" of choirs does not obstruct our perception that the participants are children, and that they *must* be children. And this, I believe, is the crucial difference between activities of either type (1) or type (2), and women's gymnastics. Top-class, open, women's gymnastics requires childlike characteristics, without declaring itself as such. It presents itself as a competition not simply for children, but rather, as a mature or adult activity, while nevertheless requiring pre-adolescent characteristics. It is *this* — the presentation as adult, as a display of unqualifiedly *human,* not child, excellence for us to view and appreciate accordingly — which renders it perverse. We do not have to guard our perception of the activity with the awareness that we are, after all, ogling *children.* We are, instead, encouraged — rather, *required* — to watch the performance as one which reveals mature, adult, qualities. In this way, our perception is to be unguarded, or unqualified. And it must be this way in order for gymnastics to have the status for viewers of being the Olympic event that it is. It would not spur the interest that it does if its status were anything else. Its success (and very existence as such an event) requires that it be considered in some sense or other as embodying the development of some mature characteristics or abilities.

Infants have some abilities which are simply absent from people of any older age. For example, if their interest could be maintained, babies could apparently do straight-leg raises all day long; and some can do all sorts of twisting and contorting of their bodies. Presumably, these "talents" could be developed to some degree. We would not do such a thing, however: (a) Even if there were interest in viewing such performances, the development and display of these abilities would clearly be exploitative (in the bad sense) of the children. And, (b) there would not, in fact, be any interest in such spectacles, largely because of the inescapable perception of them as exhibiting infantile abilities, even though they would certainly be exhibiting the pinnacle of those abilities (i.e., the winner here wouldn't win only the junior division, but would, in fact, take out the open division against all comers, as well).

I realize that there are *lots* of activities which infants or children do not do better than adults, and which are still not Olympic events simply because of that. There is more required of a physical activity for it to ascend to the height of becoming an Olympic event than that adults do it better than children. Arm-wrestling will probably never be accepted as an Olympic event. Still, my claim is not "If adults can do it better, then it is an appropriate Olympic event." Rather, the claim is, "If adults cannot do it better, or if it is not essentially an adult activity, then it is not an appropriate Olympic event." Further, I suggest that as a matter of fact, unless the activity is *perceived* as a display of adult development, then it would not be considered by an audience at large as an appropriate event to contest on such a stage.

I do not believe that my talk about immaturity or childlikeness in contrast with adult characteristics requires that I enter into an account of what makes for an *adult* characteristic anyway. I am not suggesting that a twenty-two year old sprinter or a nineteen year old swimmer must be a fully mature adult, a full-fledged candidate to run for political office. I am suggesting, however, that there is an important difference between women's gymnastics and other sports, in terms of the premium which women's gymnastics places on particularly childlike characteristics. The sport is presented as adult, the spectators are required to view it in this way. But what they are viewing are participants who are required to appear, and behave, and have attributes like little girls. I am not claiming that there is anything perverse about little girls engaging in the activity of gymnastics.[3] The perversity resides in the *design, presentation, and patronage* of the public display of the activity; not in those who participate in it. It is the marketing of girls' gymnastics as women's gymnastics which is perverse (and the marketing is essential to the sport) — the elevation of the sport of girls' gymnastics to the status of an Olympic event, an event wherein the spectator ostensibly views the fullness of human achievement, not the exploitation of a child's attributes.

---

3 I should make clear a claim which I am not advancing here: I am not claiming that the perversity stems from the fact that the participants are but children, who have not attained an "age of reason". Their performance, then, should strike us with something of the character of animals which are put through hoops. They have only little say or rational choice about it all. I do not mean to discount a claim advanced along these lines; but I am not here advancing such an argument myself. I am not claiming perversity in the name of, or as a result of, mistreatment or manipulation of children. Rather, I am claiming perversity as a result of misrepresentation and required misperception of an activity which is done by children.

Vocations and Vocations

Some people like their jobs; some people don't. Some people *really* like their jobs. A small percentage of people have vocations which are the activities they truly *want* to perform. That is, they not only like their jobs as jobs, but they like their jobs as activities that they would choose to do. They view their vocations not merely as enjoyable vocations, but as activities which they would, if they could, choose, irrespective of vocation. Simply, their vocations are things they want to do. Such a person might feel lucky (maybe even bemused) at being paid to do something that he wants to do. Or, viewed from a slightly different perspective, such a person might feel lucky that there is a market which will pay him to do this thing. Given that there is such a market, he is able to do, and get paid for doing, something which he truly wants to do. He might even think that if there were not such a market, it would be a shame that he could not afford the luxury of engaging in this activity: "Thank God that this activity which I love can be a vocation; and thank God that I can be employed in it." (This is, in fact, quite different from the norm, as illustrated in an advertisement which used to appear on Australian television, where a fellow says, "I don't live to work; I work to live", and then knocks off work to go enjoy himself.)

Notice that there are two parts to the lucky person's view of it all: First, he appreciates that a certain sort of vocation exists. (For instance, as enjoyable as it may be to some people, the activity of daydreaming is simply not a possible vocation for anyone, and most people cannot afford to while away hour after hour daydreaming.) And second, this person recognizes that he is fortunate enough to be able to engage in it as a vocation. (Although tennis-playing can be a vocation for some people, it can't be for me. As much as I might like the activity and wish that I were good enough at it to be a professional tennis player, the fact is that it is not within my capability to engage in this activity as a vocation.) Both parts of the lucky person's view have to do with his own perception of the matter and with his own preferences. It is not that he has identified some vocation as objectively preferable to or intrinsically more enjoyable than some others. Rather, he has recognized his own likes and some possibilities for himself.

The general point about people's view of themselves and their situations in various vocations may be interesting, but it is hardly earthshattering, surprising, or puzzling. The point does, however, function as a premise in a different, and I think, more puzzling point, which has to do not with satisfaction or enjoyment in one's vocation, but rather with *dissatisfaction*. One feature of the point to which I have been calling attention is simply that we all recognize that there are different strokes for different folks, and that some people are lucky enough to be able to engage in the strokes they like, as part of their vocations. Now, what about the great majority, who, to cite the television advertisement again, work to live rather than live to work? Indeed, what about them? There is nothing particularly noteworthy about them in this respect, because they are, in fact, the norm. There is nothing special to explain, nothing special to notice. *But this is not quite right.* It is apparently not right when applied to a certain group of people who are, for one reason or another, among the majority, who work to live. And it is exactly this which is the puzzle: Namely, why is it that for a certain group — but only for that certain group — which is part of the otherwise understandable, not-in-need-of-explanation majority, some sort of explanation or justification for why they are not terrifically happy in what they do for a job seems called for? Why is it that some people would seem to have to justify *not* enjoying their jobs; or, more strongly, why is it that some people would seem to have to justify not finding self-fulfilment in their vocations? Why is it that for these people, it is even seen as *morally objectionable* that their vocations are *not* activities of the sort that they would want to choose irrespective of vocation? Why is it seen (by others) as objectionable that these people's view of their situation is (merely) like most *other* people's view of *their* situations? Why is it objectionable that these people merely work to live, rather than live to work? Why is *that* regarded as objectionable? What is there about it which, to some people's eyes, warrants reproach? I will speculate at an answer to these questions. In terms of moral insights, however, it seems to me that simply noticing *that* there is this phenomenon is nearly on a par with offering an explanation of it.

Let me make all this a bit more concrete: Sam is a salesman. He views his work as drudgery. He doesn't like it at all, but it's a living. He does it solely to make money in order to do the things he wants to do. Gail is a gardener. She doesn't *dislike* her job, but gardening is not the activity she would do for enjoyment or for self-fulfilment. Frank is a farmer, and he loves it. In everything that goes along with raising a crop, he finds enjoyment and fulfilment. For him, farming is the activity he most wants to do. Frank sees himself as one of the lucky few: an activity which he greatly enjoys exists as a possible vocation, and he is able to be employed in it.

Suppose that Gail had the same view of gardening that Sam has of being a salesman (viz. that it's drudgery). There is no difficulty in imagining that; it is easily supposed that she can't stand gardening. Or, suppose that Sam had the same view of being a salesman that Frank has of being a farmer. That, too, we can imagine. Just as one could compose an appropriate soliloquy for Frank to deliver in professing his love of farming, so it would not be difficult to construct a speech for Sam about life on the road and the glory of the hard sell. Or, further, we could equally well imagine that Frank has a view of farming the same as Sam's view that selling is very unpleasant. What appears to be the case from this sort of imagining is that any vocation could fall into any category: disliked, not disliked but not enjoyed, or enjoyed for itself. Apparently, it is not the vocation itself which determines the category to which it belongs. Rather, the individual who is employed in it does the determining. It is, purely and simply, a matter of individual preference, individual likes and dislikes. So, we are neither surprised nor not surprised that some person does or does not truly enjoy her occupation. We do not think one way or the other about the fact that Gail does or does not like being a gardener.

Up to a point, all this is so. However — and it is this which I find particularly interesting — there are apparent exceptions to this way of our describing and accepting a person's regard for his job. For *some* vocations, it seems that the general view is that those who occupy them *should* not dislike them. At the very least, the people who hold such jobs should not *dislike* them, and probably those people should actually enjoy them as activities that they would otherwise choose to perform. The general view seems to be that people who hold certain sorts of jobs *should* regard themselves as among the lucky few. And not only this.

It also seems that if those people do not see themselves this way, they can be subject to something like moral disapproval or even moral reproach for not enjoying their jobs as activities that they would want to engage in, irrespective of vocation.

Now, how about some actual examples of this phenomenon? What are some actual candidates for vocations which people appear to think ought to be liked as activities by the people who are employed in them? Suppose Scott dislikes his job as a school teacher. Mike dislikes being a musician. Anne hates academia. Don does not find enjoyment in being a doctor. Helen hates being a housewife/mother. It is not hard to continue the list. Certainly there would be disagreement about whether or not to include some particular members in this list. Depending on their particular views, different people would include different members. Still, I don't think there would be any doubt that at least for most people, *some* (unspecified) vocations would belong in such a list. The interesting point does not concern what should be included in the list; rather, what is puzzling is that there could be any such list at all. Given the basic view that personal preference, rather than some intrinsic quality of a possible occupation, is what makes any vocation an enjoyable activity, why, then, should or could there be a list of vocations which *ought* to be liked as activities by the people who are engaged in them?

Let me first say something about the sense which can or cannot be made of the 'ought' here. If there is not some pertinent feature of the activity itself, the only sense which can be made of this 'ought' is one which refers to the people engaging in the activity: i.e., "*these people* ought to find the activity attractive"; not "the *activity* ought to be seen as attractive". These people ought to like the activity because of something about themselves, rather than because of something about the activity itself. Still, this needs some clearing up. No one thinks that everyone ought to like the activity of schoolteaching, musicianing, or doctoring. So, if one judges that Mike ought to like being a musician, it must be because of something about Mike, not something about all people or just anybody, and not something about musicianing itself. Further, it is not that the moral judge here must think that Mike has some feature which suits him to being a musician: No; we would not necessarily have thought that Mike had missed his natural calling if he had become something other than a musician. And it is not as though anyone would have thought ill of him had he become something else. Rather, it is only when Mike is *being a musician who does not like the activity of musicianing* that one might have anything at all harsh to say about him in relation to his vocation. It is only here where Mike could well find himself viewed with something like moral disapproval — moral disapproval for not enjoying a particular vocation.

There is one explanation which might explain all the features of such a case, but which, nevertheless, simply cannot be correct — I just *know* that it cannot be correct, but it *is* worth mentioning. It is this:

> The cases which evoke the response of moral disapproval are cases where both (i) the vocation in question is generally *so dis*tasteful to most people, and (ii) the person involved *chose* it, knowing of its general distaste. So, inasmuch as he was aware of the general regard for it and chose it anyway, he deserves what he got. He made his bed; now he must lie in it. Not only that, but how dare he now voice his dislike of it.

He must not only lie in his bed, but lie in it uncomplainingly. Perhaps he ought, in fact, even to lie in it enjoyingly.

Now, although this is obviously not the correct explanation, it does, nevertheless, have two elements which, in one way or another, have a place in what I believe to be the correct explanation. First, it makes reference to a person's having chosen a vocation. Second, the indignant "how dare you" is indeed a part of the response of the moral disapprovers.

The fact that Cheryl chose to do what she is doing is at least some reason for the rest of us to think that she now does not dislike it. By itself, however, this does not involve or call for any *evaluation* of her not liking it. Further, it might be that some jobs are, in fact, generally thought to be genuine candidates for likeable activities, or at least that the activities involved in them would, as a matter of fact, have positive appeal to a greater number of people than would the activities involved in other vocations. If that is so, then somebody's having chosen one of *these* vocations and now not liking it might seem to be more telling. How dare she choose to do and now be doing this thing which, apparently, lots of people would find enjoyable in itself, and yet she not like it! Still, the move to the "how dare you" evaluation seems an odd one. Why not, instead, "pity the poor creature who chose the inviting occupation and now does not take enjoyment in it"?

Could it be that something about a person's *choosing* an occupation which appears to most people as an *enjoyable activity* can be central to the explanation of why this person is disapproved of if he does not fancy himself among the "lucky few"? What is this person's crime which leads to the judgment of disapproval? It cannot be simply that he does not enjoy something: we certainly do not disapprove of someone who, even though he can easily afford it, does not like lobster mornay. Nor can it be simply that he suffers as a result of his own choice: people do not disapprove of someone's discovering, as a result of ordering it from the menu, that he does not like lobster mornay. Although Bill might not enjoy his career, and might even suffer as a result of mis-choosing his career, this dissatisfaction or suffering fails to furnish an explanation or a justification of the general disapproval of him.

Perhaps the "crime" is one of ingratitude:

> "There you are in a position to be truly enjoying your
> vocation (you chose it, and it appears to most people
> to be an enjoyable activity), and what do you do? You
> up and have a terrible time! How dare you do that,
> you ingrate!"

This is closer, I think. The ingratitude is not that of failing to appreciate the particular fruits from the particular vocation. Rather, the offense of ingratitude is directed against the *position* that Bill was *privileged* to have, from which he could make a choice in the first place. It is in virtue of one's position or vantage point for choosing, not in virtue of the resultant chosen vocation itself, that the agent is, as it were, held *liable* for not finding enjoyment or fulfilment in the chosen vocation. One's lack of enjoyment is seen as a sign of being ungrateful for being one of the few who are in a position to choose among a variety of vocations, each of which presents an apparently enjoyable activity. The ingratitude is displayed in the carelessness with which this person chose a vocation. Bill did not take care enough to procure for himself what he could have. There he was. He could choose for himself among a myriad of possibilities. More careful attention to the choice and he could have found something which is not even a *possibility* for most people. He could have chosen as a vocation an activity in which he would find enjoyment and self-fulfilment. But what did he do? Rather than cherishing and exploiting this very special opportunity and so acting in the way he was beholden to act, he botched it; he frittered away a choice. Through failure to appreciate his special opportunity, he ended up like most people. He ended up like those people who did not have the possibility of so easily choosing well for themselves. "If *I'd* had your opportunity, *I* would have done well for *my*self."

This would give more bitter bite to the advice to an offspring, "Choose wisely, my child!" It would mean not only that the choice is important and that you might suffer as a result of a wrong choice. It would also indicate that with the wrong choice, you could, in addition, be subject to a harsh *moral* judgment.

The moral disapproval is not aimed directly at one's lack of enjoyment of the vocation. Neither is it aimed directly at one's *choosing* a vocation. Its target is the station from which one chose; and it finds its justification there, as well — if, in fact, it has any justification at all. Perhaps it is much the same as the reaction (or at least part of the reaction) to the prodigal son. It is not because of his ultimate poverty that he is disapproved of. Looking only at his poverty, who would feel anything but pity? Rather, it is that he is seen to have had it all, including the perspective requisite to choose in ways which would benefit and satisfy himself. He is seen to have had that vantage point, and he is also seen to have blown it for himself. Maybe someone would be generous enough to pity him. A more likely reaction would be to think that he is at best foolish, and worthy of a kick in the pants. He did not *appreciate* the position from which he, unlike most people, was able to get himself into a vocation. Indeed, if he had appreciated the position from which he was fortunate to be able to choose, he would have done better for himself than he did. His crime is ingratitude or lack of appreciation of the position, the vantage point, from which he was lucky enough to be able to choose. This, I think, is the central, or principal, explanation of the phenomenon of some people being judged morally harshly for not finding true enjoyment or fulfilment in their chosen vocations. The explanation focuses on the chooser of the vocation, and not on the vocation itself.

Another explanation is also possible. Even if some particular moral judge did not feel moral disapproval in the case or for the reasons I have just discussed, he still might morally disapprove in either of two other cases, where in addition to the agent's choosing, the judge has some significant regard for the particular vocation which the agent chose. Contributing toward the moral disapproval of the poor soul who does not take pleasure in his vocation may well be the feeling, on the part of one who is judging morally, that this person's particular vocation is one which numerous people clamor after. In terms of numbers alone, he would have to be considered one of the fortunate ones to land the (statistically-speaking) desirable occupation. So, it might well strike someone as reproachable that this fellow does not appreciate that thing from which so many others are excluded. This explanation focuses not only on the person's choosing the vocation but also on the apparent desirability and exclusivity of the vocation itself.

There is another, more interesting, possible explanation which warrants comment. This one, too, focuses on the vocation itself as well as on the choosing. However, rather than picking up on the desirability and exclusivity of the vocation, this explanation would look to a different type of characteristic of the vocation, the characteristic of being an end in itself, as distinguished from being a means to a further end, or a "service activity". Early in this discussion, I indicated that it is possible (or at least we can imagine) that any vocation at all might be regarded by *someone* as an activity that that person really wants to engage in for its own sake, i.e., as an end in itself. Still, some vocations more than others seem to be more easily suited to be candidates for being ends in themselves, rather than leading to something further or being performed for the sake of something other than themselves. And, some vocations seem more obviously to be means toward other goals. These vocations are "service activities", in that their rational is for the sake of allowing for or making possible something besides themselves. They "serve" other activities or purposes. Although bricklaying may be an activity in which someone finds self-fulfilment, it would seem more obviously and more usually to be an activity performed to serve some other purpose — for example, to provide a comfortable house.[1] To say that some activity is a service vocation is by no means to say that it is not an honorable or proper or even prestigious vocation. It is only to say that it is

---

1 In the movie *The Hustler*, Fast Eddie Felson (Paul Newman) provides a lovely, if extreme, speculative description of what bricklaying would feel like by someone engaged in it as an end in itself. And, he offers the same sort of description of his own feelings when he's at the top of his game in shooting pool:

not surprising (let alone reproachable) that someone engaged in it as a vocation does not find self-fulfilment in it and does not regard it as an activity he would like to engage in regardless of vocation. In this respect, one might regard such noble professions as lawyering and doctoring as service vocations. Of course, a person might be attracted to the beauty of the structure and workings of the law. Or, a person might be an altruist, finding self-fulfilment in providing other people's physical well-being. For such people, perhaps, the practice of law or medicine would be an end in itself, rather than a vocation for the purpose of something else. Still, these vocations, like other service vocations, are generally undertaken for some purpose other than for themselves alone. They service other activities or ends, and the practitioner is rewarded most commonly not through finding self-fulfilment, but through being well-paid.

"anything can be great. ANYTHING can be great. I don't care. . . bricklaying can be great, if a guy knows — if he knows what he's doing and why and can make it come off. And when I'm going — I mean when I'm really going — I feel like a . . . like a jockey must feel: he's sittin' up there on his horse, he's got all that speed and that power underneath him, he's comin' into the stretch, the pressure's on him . . . and he knows . . . just feels . . . when to let it go and how much . . . 'cause he's got everything workin' for him: timing, touch. It's a great feeling, boy, it's a . . . real great feeling. When you're right. Like all of a sudden, I got oil in my arm. pool cue's part of me. Ya know, it's a . . . pool cue, it's got nerves in it: it's a piece a wood, it's got nerves in it. [Ya] feel the roll of those balls . . . ya don't have to look, ya just know. You make shots that nobody's ever made before. And ya play that game the way . . . nobody's ever played it before."

Now suppose that Fran regards a certain vocation as a candidate for being a non-service activity. And suppose that she regards Bill as having *chosen* this activity *as such*. Suppose further that she now sees Bill as less than satisfied with his choice. It is here, I suggest, that the conditions are ripe for Fran to morally disapprove of Bill. Bill chose to be a musician, an activity which Fran perceives to be (at least potentially) an end in itself. So, Fran sees Bill as one of the lucky few who has as his chosen vocation an activity which is a candidate to provide self-fulfilment. In this respect, Bill's choice is seen as, literally, self-indulgent. He chose an activity which leads only to itself; and that is a situation which Fran believes that Bill should certainly have appreciated in choosing this vocation. Everyone is looking for self-fulfilment and enjoyment of an activity in itself. Bill was in a position to identify such an activity, and he had the opportunity to pursue it and to be supported in his pursuit of it. If someone finds Bill's dissatisfaction reproachable, then, it might well be because of the relationship in which Bill stands (or stood) toward his vocation, a relationship considerably different from and more privileged than the norm: he could choose an activity expressly for the purpose of his self-fulfilment and enjoyment alone, and he could be paid to pursue it. If he botched it, who is he to complain? He could have adopted a safer, less self-indulgent strategy in the beginning. What he is suffering now is the result of his own careless self-indulgence. The moral judge might disapprove of him for precisely this.

This discussion about vocations has had two targets. First, I have called attention to what I take to be an odd phenomenon: the moral evaluation of a select group of people for being dissatisfied in their jobs. Second, regardless of whether there is adequate, or even reasonable, *justification* for this moral disapproval, I have speculated at an *explanation* of it. Centrally, the explanation concerns one individual's being perceived as having been in a rather privileged position from which to choose any vocation for himself at all. Further, I have suggested, there appear to be some cases which have significant features which need not be present in the central explanation. Even if some particular moral judge did not feel moral disapproval in the central case alone, he might still feel it in one of the other cases, both of which involve a perception of the status or quality of the particular vocation as well as of the chooser of that vocation.

The Last Word

It is a moral failing — at least a serious breach of etiquette — to insist on always having the last word, or the final say, on all and sundry topics. The most common species of this failing is exhibited by a person's insisting that it will be *his* view or opinion or pronouncement about some particular matter which will close the discussion about that matter. No matter how hard others might try to gain the last word or to gain this person's assent to a view which *they* express, the true insistor-on-having-the-last-word will always have something to add or to alter, so that his word will be the last one. People like this can drive you nuts. And, people like this are not difficult to find (if, for whatever reason, you should ever actually want to go looking for one of them). They know everything, they know all the fine points and considerations which are worth knowing, and they know what it is that need not be known or considered. And, of course, they will insist on telling you all of this. They are members of the class of know-all bastards. But this, the most common species, is not the species to which I want to call attention here. The insistor-on-having-the-last-word which I have in mind is not concerned about expressing an *opinion* or a *viewpoint,* but is, rather, concerned about expressing *gratitude.* This person insists on expressing gratitude and expressing it in such a way that the one to whom the gratitude is expressed might well feel that a "debt" has been "repaid" — both of which notions should, in fact, be absent from dealings, or transactions, of this kind. Or, perhaps it would be better to say, this person will, by his behavior, transform something which is *not* a transaction (a bit of non-transactional interpersonal behavior) into a transaction, thereby perverting its nature and not allowing the other party the status which would be appropriate to him. I do not think that the insistor *tries* to do this; but he does indeed do it, nevertheless.

> Robert: Thanks very much.
>
> Ethel: Really, it was nothing.
>
> Robert: No; you went out of your way. Thanks.
>
> Ethel: No trouble. I would have done the same for anyone.
>
> Robert: Oh yes it was. It was very thoughtful of you.
>
> Ethel: . . .

Somewhere this exchange must stop. And, one of these people (probably Robert) *ought* to allow it to stop, *ought* to allow the other person the last word.

The phenomenon of the last word need not be as drawn out as that between Robert and Ethel; and it need not involve words at all:

> One day, burglars were trying to break into Jean's house while she was at work. Bill, a neighbor but not really an acquaintance of Jean's, happened to notice the breaking in, and phoned the police, who arrived very quickly and thwarted the burglary. When she learned of this, Jean was quick to thank Bill for his

neighborly concern and civic-minded action. Bill accepted Jean's thanks, adding that he was happy to have been able to help. Jean then phoned a florist and had a gratitude-arrangement of flowers, a hamper of goodies, and a thank-you card sent to Bill. (Jean secured for herself the last word.)

Or:

Chuck's car wouldn't start, the battery was dead. Greg, a passing motorist, noticed Chuck's difficulty, stopped, and offered Chuck a jump-start. Chuck happily accepted Greg's kind offer, and the car started straight away. Chuck expressed his thanks profusely, and he then offered to pay Greg something for his trouble (this would get him the last word, and it would turn the whole act of helping into a transaction). Greg said "no" to the offer of payment — he remained gracious in declining Chuck's offer, however. When Greg arrived home, he discovered that Chuck had slipped $5 into his jacket pocket. (Chuck secured for himself the last word.)

Jean and Chuck have insisted on having the last word, and they are wrong to do it. (It would be possible to tell a different story, according to which Chuck would *not* be wrong in offering payment. I'll return to that difficulty later.) Let me step away from this level of discussion for a moment.

Philosophers have spoken a fair bit and there has been a substantial amount of philosophical debate about a person's moral duty to aid other people.[1] However, there has been very little discussion about what would be a proper response, or proper behavior in general, by the one who has been aided. Let me call attention to an area in which philosophers have, to some very small extent, addressed a problem very similar to that of the "last word" in the above examples and similar also to the general issue of how an individual should respond to assistance. There has been some philosophical and some legal discussion over whether it would be possible — and, if possible, then whether it would be desirable — to legally require or encourage some degree of good samaritanism, or rescue or assistance of people in distress. One possible way of legally encouraging one person to come to another's aid would be to implement a formal system of providing compensation to someone who comes to someone else's aid — basically, paying good samaritans for their trouble and time away from whatever else they might otherwise have been doing. (Perhaps this could be achieved by requiring that each of us be covered by a compensation-to-rescuer insurance policy, so that each of us is, in one way or another, required to compensate someone who rescues us.) In canvassing some central arguments for and against the presence of a formal apparatus to encourage or require rescue, A. M. Honoré touches on this possibility, coupled with a requirement that the

---

1 Even when their actual moral theories do not seem to require such behavior, some philosophers have gone to great lengths — or better, "contortions" — to try to convince us that there is such a duty and that their theories do, in fact, require it. Immanuel Kant and his requirement of a duty of beneficence is, perhaps, the clearest example of such a contortionist.

rescuer be compensated, or that compensation come more or less automatically to the rescuer — a setup in which a rescuer's receiving compensation is virtually unavoidable.[2] Honoré agrees that *compelling* a rescuer to be compensated would clearly be a bad thing. It would, for instance, preempt the possibility for a rescuer to accept virtue as its own reward. Compelling him to accept compensation would fail to respect the rescuer's moral idealism. A virtuous act done for payment — or even a virtuous act for which one is paid, regardless of whether the prospect of payment figured in the agent's decision to perform the act — has a different character from a virtuous act done for its own sake. Or, we could say (as a different point) that inasmuch as the rescuer is the good guy in all this (it is *his* action which might warrant praise), it is only fair that he should be allowed the last word, if that is what he wants. To insist on the rescuer's being compensated is to take away from him this option to have the final say on the matter.

And, this is exactly what is wrong with Jean's and Chuck's behavior. They recognize that their "rescuers" have done good things, but they fail to accord them the status that they deserve. Jean and Chuck will not allow Bill's and Greg's actions to be virtuous for virtue's sake alone; they will not allow those actions

---

2 "Law, Morals and Rescue" in *The Good Samaritan and the Law*, ed. James M. Ratcliffe (New York: Doubleday & Co., Inc., 1966), pp. 225-242. (Reprinted in *Philosophy of Law*, 2nd Edition, ed. Joel Feinberg and Hyman Gross [Belmont, California: Wadsworth, 1980], pp. 440-446, particularly 443ff.)

to be purely altruistic. Or, perhaps it is better to say that Jean and Chuck themselves refuse to *view* Bill's and Greg's actions in this way.   Jean and Chuck cannot actually preclude the actions having that virtuous character, but they can, as it were, attempt to give them a different (and possibly unpleasant) flavor. This is not to say that Jean and Chuck are bad guys or that, in behaving as they did, their motives are ignoble. Most likely, it would be quite the contrary. It could well be that on moral or, perhaps, religious grounds, they believe that virtue should be rewarded. And, in the cases at hand, they are simply trying to do the rewarding themselves. If this is so, then it is not their motives, but rather their insensitivity which is the subject of criticism. They are insensitive to the desire (and to the entitlement) of their rescuers to have the acts treated differently, and to have the character of those acts respected in the way in which the rescuers think appropriate. If Bill and Greg do not want rewards, they might still want their acts to be appreciated for what they are (or at least not to be misunderstood). And if this is so, we can see that rescuers might reasonably even be *offended* by rewards which are foisted upon them by those toward whom they were altruistic. Perhaps it does not matter to Bill and Greg. Perhaps they can simply brush off Jean's and Chuck's inappropriate responses as uncalled for and unnecessary. But, it is at least understandable if they are, to some degree, offended. And, regardless of whether they themselves are offended, we can still say that (given this story of why Bill and Greg did what they did), Jean's and Chuck's responses to their actions were not merely unnecessary; they also represent a failure on Jean and Chuck's part to accord a morally significant action its proper status, or character, and to allow its agent the status which he has (or deserves). If Jean and Chuck do recognize that Bill and

Greg have done something good, and if they recognize what it is that they are grateful for, then they simply should *not* continue on to present their rescuers with rewards. Instead, they must allow their rescuers' actions to have the character that the rescuers themselves desire; and Jean and Chuck must themselves be gracious in *accepting* what has been given to them. They cannot insist on making it the case that it is the rescuers who, in the end, must *accept* something given to *them*.

To foist rewards onto their rescuers is, among other things, selfish or self-centered behavior. It is to insist on securing for oneself the position of setting the terms of the interaction. If, for instance, one believed that in some moral, religious, or psychological sense, "it is better to give than to receive", then Jean and Chuck might be seen as grabbing for themselves a piece of the better, "giving", pie, rather than allowing their rescuers the full pastry for themselves. Characterizing their behavior as selfish is, of course, ironic inasmuch as, surely, they were trying to perform acts which were not morally *required*, but were instead going that extra mile. They would see themselves as doing something which was morally nice but not mandatory. What I am suggesting, however, is that it is precisely this which is *objectionable* about their behavior. At the least, they have revealed a very limited, particularly self-centered perception of the moral features of the interaction.

It would be easy to tell a different story about Greg's helping Chuck, according to which it would not be an offence for Chuck either to offer or even to insist upon paying some rescuer for the assistance. (I think it would be more difficult to tell a comparable different story for Bill's helping Jean. More likely, I think, is that given even the morally most favorable scenario for Jean, her behavior will have more the character of gilding the lily than of going the extra mile. And, I think this is because Jean's response — the flowers — is nothing *but* a further display of gratitude, whereas Chuck's — the $5 — has more the character of a pay-off as well. And, given the right story, a pay-off per se could be appreciated by Greg or could be appropriate in some other way. But that would be a different story.)

Recognizing, then, that different stories are possible, how should a potential gratitude-displayer decide on the proper way to show his gratitude? How is he supposed to know which type of rescuer he is dealing with — the one for whom a pay-off would be appropriate, or the one who would like to have the last word himself? I think that there is no formula or mechanical way of answering this question. And, I also think that it is a fair example of an important claim which Aristotle made about virtuous behavior of any kind, namely, that in the end (at the point where the prospective agent appraises the situation with an eye to acting properly), it is a matter of "perception": One must simply *see* the situation for what it is; one cannot calculate what it is or what he should do.[3] To say that it is a matter of perception in this sense is not to say that in whatever way any person happens to see the situation, that perception must be correct. There can certainly be misperceptions. That is exactly the difficulty: In these situations, indeed, there is a right thing to do and there is a wrong thing to do. The point about perception

---

3 Aristotle, *Nicomachean Ethics*, e.g., $1103^{b}30$ - $1104^{a}9$ (Bk.2, chap.2); $1107^{a}27$-32 (Bk.2, chap.9); $1143^{b}2$-14 (Bk.6, chap.13).

is a point about how one comes to recognize which is which in a particular situation. It is not a point about what *makes* right right and what *makes* wrong wrong. What one *can* do in a situation where the last word and gratitude can be an issue, then, is to recognize, as Jean apparently does not, that it *is* such a situation and that it does, in fact, present an issue. Further, one can recognize, as a rule of thumb, that the rescuer (the one performing the action for which the other is grateful) is *entitled* to the last word if he wants it. And, perhaps we could even go a bit further and suggest that there is a *presumption* that the rescuer would indeed want it; so that unless there is something which *displaces* the presumption in any particular situation, the rescuer should be accorded the last word.[4]

If, in recognizing the nature of the situation, the gratitude-displayer makes the wrong call about (i.e., misperceives) what would be the proper response in the particular situation, then he has erred morally. But that error is not of the same magnitude as that of failing altogether to recognize that the situation is, in fact, one in which there is a genuine moral consideration with respect to the last word.

Some people approach all interpersonal situations armed with a principle such as "I pay my own way." They shouldn't adopt this approach; and not merely because it is bad strategy. Approaching all interpersonal situations in this way has the effect (whether or not it is intended) of preempting the require-

---

4 I suppose that whether you think that there should be this presumption depends on what your view is of humanity.

ment that the agent *consider* the situation as involving some *issue* of the last word. It fails to recognize that there is something to be sorted out with respect to the particular circumstances.

Adopting the "I pay my own way" strategy would, of course, allow one to avoid the position of indecision or of having to decide the issue of the last word in each particular situation. Further, the precept "I pay my own way", just like, for instance, "Neither a borrower nor a lender be", might be offered as an expression of one's self-sufficiency, which should be appreciated as a moral *asset*. However, I suggest, in circumstances involving gratitude — situations in which someone has come to someone else's aid — the moral price that one must pay for the illusion (or self-deception) of self-sufficiency is *actual selfishness*.[5] Refusing to respect another's altruism or beneficence and claiming for oneself the satisfaction of "having settled the account" can hardly count as being virtuous.

We might maintain that an approach to life on the order of "I pay my own way" or "Neither a borrower nor a lender be" would in any case be a particularly coarse outlook, one which does not allow for the full possibility of humanity in interpersonal relations: After all, receiving, as well as giving, is an important aspect of interpersonal behavior, which itself provides the largest arena for moral behavior. To deny the possibility of "proper" behavior with respect to *either* of these aspects is not at all praiseworthy or noble in itself. *Gracious* receipt and *gracious*

---

5 In such a situation, self-sufficiency can be no more than illusory, inasmuch as, ex hypothesi, these situations are ones which involve gratitude *for assistance.*

provision of assistance are not merely virtues which a person can have if that person is unable to pay his own way. Being *gracious* in providing for and in receiving from others are facets of human behavior which have moral value not merely if one is unable to make it on his own. Both aspects of graciousness are integral parts of human (*human*) relations. A person's never allowing anyone to assist him (let alone *asking* for assistance) denies others the possibility of functioning toward this person in a way in which they can be gracious; and it also preempts for the person himself a mode of being gracious. One might make this point *in general* with respect to such aphorisms about self-sufficiency; and, by itself, that could be damning of someone who claimed to conduct his affairs accordingly. But, when such expressions of devotion to self-sufficiency are offered in the context of a situation which calls for gratitude, they are self-deceitful, as well. The person who offers them has already instanced a degree of *absence* of self-sufficiency, inasmuch as someone has already come to his aid (finding him *not* to be self-sufficient). For the person now to insist that self-sufficiency requires him to pay up is utterly to misperceive the situation. Self-sufficiency is not at all at issue; gratitude is.